CLASSIC ROCK
DRUMMERS

BY KEN MICALLEF and DONNIE MARSHALL

Backbeat
Books

An Imprint of Hal Leonard Corporation
New York

Photos:
Courtesy Michael Ochs Archives.com
Except:
Mitch Mitchell: Courtesy Jill Gibson/Michael Ochs Archives.com
Levon Helm: Courtesy Joel Axelrad/Michael Ochs Archives.com

Layout by Stephen Ramirez

Library of Congress Cataloging-in-Publication Data is available upon request.
ISBN 10: 0-87930-907-5
ISBN 13: 978-0-87930-907-7

Published in 2007 by
Backbeat Books (an imprint of Hal Leonard Corporation)
19 West 21st Street,
New York, NY 10010

Printed in the United States of America

www.backbeatbooks.com

The book is dedicated to Mickey and Jim Marshall, and John and Myra Micallef

CONTENTS

INTRODUCTION

 All the great drummers, regardless of style or genre, have a unique voice on the instrument, which is their signature sound, one that any student of their music can recognize in a second. Fans of John Bonham can spot the tumbling tom fills of Led Zeppelin's "Stairway to Heaven" in five clicks of an iPod. Similarly, the turbulent rhythmic conceptions of The Police's Stewart Copeland are as memorable as Sting's adenoidal howl. Keith Moon's exploding wall of toms and cymbals, Ringo Starr's laconic beats and tom fills, Ian Paice's burning single-stroke rolls and funk-charged beats—these are the sonic trademarks of a genre that radio programmers label classic rock, but more important, they are invaluable artistic statements that inspire us to create our own style, our own voice, and our own unique way of playing music.

What better way to understand a drummer's identity than to analyze his style through the songs that made him famous? *Classic Rock Drummers* focuses on the patterns, grooves, fills, and eccentricities of the most lauded rock drummers of the twentieth century. Through detailed analyses of their playing style and specific tracks, including such areas as time conception, influences, snare drum technique, meter construction, and independence, we hope to shed light on what can be a surprisingly deceptive art form.

Everyone has seen The Muppets' Animal maniacally bashing a toy drum, his arms flailing and his eyes bugging out, and for many that is the lasting symbol of the classic rock drummer. A beast. An animal. A nonthinking pounder worthy of jokes and amusement. But without a great drummer, you will never have a great band. It all begins and ends with the groove. As in jazz, where every musical innovation involves a marriage of melody and rhythm, classic rock was a furnace where melodic (usually guitar) innovation was matched with percussive rhythmic inventions of equal weight and value. Jimmy Page's searing guitar riffs would have meant little without the support, inspiration, and interaction of John Bonham. Ginger Baker founded Cream, and his jazz oriented-approach pushed Eric Clapton to greater heights of self-expression than he had previously imagined. Jimi Hendrix is judged as the greatest rock guitarist ever—his explorations were launched by Mitch Mitchell's jazz-infused thunder. Rhythm and melody are the parallel points that form the basis of composition, and the great drummers think in both regards.

Each chapter of *Classic Rock Drummers* includes a brief biography, setup information, style and technical analysis, and a selected listening discography, as well as an audio CD with accompanying music notation. Playing along with the audio examples will help you match the feel of the grooves, and should inspire you to hear the originals in all their splendor. Follow the count-ins before each example, and listen to each track many times before you attempt to play it. Become familiar with the attitude of each track, such as how John Bonham pushes the beat in the track styled on Led Zeppelin's "Rock and Roll" or the manic groove and tom drops in the example modeled on The Police's "Roxanne." As always, achieving the correct feel is more important than playing flashy fills; the former will keep you employed, while trying to master the latter may only leave you frustrated.

By understanding the history and methodology behind each drummer, you can better understand his rhythmic choices for the respective songs. Perhaps we can never totally plumb the depths of someone as mercurial as Keith Moon or as self-effacing as Ringo Starr, but close-up, bar-by-bar examinations of their signature songs can form a basis for deeper understanding.

The music of the classic rock drummers is ubiquitous today, from TV commercials to Internet pop-ups to wizened classic rock radio itself. But this music is classic for a reason that goes beyond commerce. It is the result of the original rock-and-roll spark, from an era when the music was raw and dangerous and its musicians ruled the world like Roman gladiators. Join us as we enter their world, learn the essentials of their style, and live to retell the tale anew.

DRUM KEY

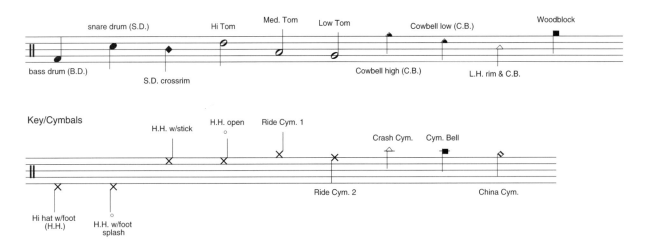

CHAPTER 1
Ginger Baker

He looked like a disheveled character from a Dickens novel, wrote poetry that was profane, pornographic, or both, and his limber jazz-rock drumming (featuring rock's very first extended drum solo) was the springboard for the world's first heavy-metal power trio, Cream.

Ginger Baker had a reputation as a wild-eyed, drug-taking, drink-imbibing madman, but his drumming expressed the soul of a true English poet. Full of character, style, and wit, his work on such classic Cream singles as "White Room," "Strange Brew," "Badge," and "Sunshine of Your Love" is the stuff of rock legend, and deservedly so. Baker blew hot winds of jazz improvisation through '60s blues-rock as no drummer in the history of music before him, but he also composed perfect pop drum parts replete with signature drum fills and beats. His 16th-note tom fills in any number of Cream classics (such as "Badge," "White Room," and "Those Were the Days") are as memorable as any Eric Clapton guitar solo, and his mastery of rhythms as diverse as African polyrhythms and blues shuffles was without parallel. Baker was the drum innovator who created the modern drum solo, in "Toad," and though his reputation was soon overshadowed by the all-powerful John Bonham, the pantheon of contemporary drummers from metal, fusion, and rock owe their very existence to Baker's trailblazing work with Cream.

BIOGRAPHY

Born Peter Edward Baker in Lewisham, London, on August 19, 1939, young "Ginger," as he was called, soon became interested in cycling and the arts. The trumpet was his first instrument, which he played in the local Air Training Corp band. Inspired by the high-handed rudiments and flashy execution of the Corp's drummer, Ginger soon began rattling his parent's brains by banging pots and pans with knives and forks. Making his own set from Perspex (acrylic), Ginger taught himself how to play and, surprisingly enough, at the age of 16 landed a job with Bob Wallis's Storyville Jazz Band, which offered the budding musician his first year on the road.

An avid listener, Ginger was inspired by all the trad jazz greats of the day, including Baby Dodds (particularly his *Talking & Drum Solos* 78s), Zutty Singleton, Big Sid Catlett, Louis Bellson, Art Blakey (Baker would battle the famed bop drummer at the 1972 Olympics, captured on *The Album* [ITM]), and, most important, Max Roach. In later years, Ginger would seem to apply Roach's dry tuning and airy time feel to his work with Cream.

Even though Baker was an uncontrollable, unconventional presence in most bands, beneath his gruff exterior lay a drum innovator biding his time while looking for the perfect break. At one point he even played Irish music with a 16-piece big band, covering Irish jigs and Gaelic music with the same intensity he brought to his trad jazz gigs.

Ginger jammed with many bands in London's nascent 1960s jazz scene, other musicians recognizing his skill but nonetheless finding his explosive, unpredictable demeanor less than pleasant. During this period he met veteran English drummer Phil Seaman, who introduced Ginger to African rhythms, as well as the dangerous pleasures of narcotics and alcohol.

In 1962, recommended by the then-departing Charlie Watts, Ginger took a left turn into the R&B scene and joined Alexis Korner's Blues Incorporated. A year later he would become a member of the all-important Graham Bond Organisation, which also featured bassist Jack Bruce and guitarist John McLaughlin. Graham, Jack, and Ginger would often jam as a trio with tremendous results, even if the bassist and drummer would end many gigs with vicious physical attacks that would seem to seal their fate as arch-enemies. (In one particularly violent brawl Bruce destroyed Ginger's Perspex set while Baker bounced sticks off the bassist's head). Though Graham Bond was the leader of the GBO, it is widely held that Baker actually ran the band, thus explaining Bruce's abrupt dismissal from this most popular of UK R&B groups.

In early 1966 Baker witnessed a performance of the hotly tipped John Mayall's Bluesbreakers, featuring guitarist Eric Clapton. Ginger sat in with the band that evening, and afterward convinced Clapton to join a band he was intent on forming. Eric agreed with one catch—that a certain bassist be included in the trio: Jack Bruce. It was decided that improvisation would be Cream's calling card, that they would create melodies and rhythms and then explore the music through their collective love of jamming.

Baker was easily the most exciting drummer of the day, though his 25-minute solos were not everyone's idea of a musical event. That would soon change when Cream debuted at the Windsor Jazz & Blues Festival in July 1966 and quickly became the most explosive, must-see band of the mid '60s.

On the strength of a string of hit singles and incendiary live performances, Cream quickly became the world's first supergroup, selling out halls across the globe. Each member was a master of his instrument, prodding and pushing

CHECKLIST ✓

❑ Drums
1960s Ludwig silver-sparkle double-bass-drum kit, Drum Workshop

❑ Condition
New

❑ Sticks
Zildjian 7A Ginger Baker Signature model

❑ Setup
Sits slightly high off kit, legs angled down

❑ Effects
Mallets, large gong, tympani, congas, cowbell

❑ Feel
Weight of groove light yet propulsive, very slippery and syncopated, explosions on demand

❑ Signature traits
Slipping, sliding time feel marked by pointed, rollicking beat; dragging tom-tom fills; inventive use of flams; bashing cymbals; off-beat hi-hat integration; innovative full-set groove patterns; military-inspired snare-drum technique; pioneering bass-drum and double-bass-drum technique; incredible soloing facility; flatly angled tom-toms tuned to an oddly resonant thud

❑ Influences
Alton Red, Phil Seaman, Max Roach, Louis Bellson, Baby Dodds, Big Sid Catlett, Elvin Jones

❑ Overall approach
A '50s-jazz-inspired approach to '60s rock marked by a loose-limbed time feel, flam-informed drum fills, innovative drum solos, and the general air of an ingenious wildman on the skins

SELECTED DISCOGRAPHY

With Cream:
Fresh Cream
Disraeli Gears
Wheels of Fire
Goodbye,
Royal Albert Hall: London May 2-3-5-6 2005

With Blind Faith:
Blind Faith

With Masters of Reality:
Sunrise on the Sufferbus

Solo albums:
Ginger Baker's Air Force
Going Back Home
Coward of the County
Ginger Baker's African Force

RECOMMENDED CUTS

"Toad" *(live version, Wheels of Fire)*
"Swlabr" *(Disraeli Gears)*
"Tales of Brave Ulysses" *(Disraeli Gears)*
"Cat's Squirrel" *(Fresh Cream)*
"Born Under a Bad Sign" *(Wheels of Fire)*
"White Room" *(Wheels of Fire)*
"Badge" *(Goodbye)*
"Rollin' and Tumblin'" *(Fresh Cream)*
"Sitting on Top of the World" *(Wheels of Fire)*
"Crossroads" *(Wheels of Fire)*
"Strange Brew" *(Disraeli Gears)*
"Pressed Rat and Warthog" *(Wheels of Fire)*
"Deserted Cities of the Heart" *(Wheels of Fire)*

the envelope with extended improvisations that transformed blues classics like "Spoonful" (Willie Dixon), "Crossroads" (Robert Johnson), "Rollin' and Tumblin'" (Muddy Waters), and "Sitting on Top of the World" (Howlin' Wolf) into inspired and at times bombastic jam sessions where everyone soloed to the extreme, not the least, Baker. Of course, his feature was "Toad," in which he artfully crammed everything he knew into a barrage of double-bass-drum combinations, flam assaults, cymbal forays, and tumbling tom expressions. (The song, complete with Ginger's soaring solo, was resurrected for Martin Scorcese's 1995 gangster epic, *Casino*).

Though they were at the vanguard of the psychedelic '60s, Cream was destined to fly high and burn out fast, lasting only two years. By the group's last tour, they were not only staying in different hotel rooms, but in different hotels. Baker and Clapton would reunite in another multi-platinum-selling band, Blind Faith, which included organist Steve Winwood and bassist Rick Grech. Blind Faith recorded only one self-titled album, which included Baker's spirited 15-minute drum-solo track, "Do What You Like." Blind Faith trumped Cream, lasting only six months.

Baker went on to form his own bands, including Ginger Baker's Air Force and the Baker-Gurvitz Army Band. In those outfits he was free to explore his growing interest in African music, which culminated in his move to Nigeria in 1970, where he built what became a popular recording studio (recording Fela Kuti and Paul McCartney, among others). But before that, Ginger appeared on George Harrison's *All Things Must Pass*, his rhythmic shenanigans totally freaking out the quiet Beatle. While in Nigeria, Baker also formed and recorded Salt, which included local Nigerian musicians and former members of Air Force.

By 1982 the music business and his perpetual drug habit had gotten the best of Baker, and he left Africa for Italy, where he taught a few students and spent most of his time tending an olive grove.

He also shook his habit once and for all. Re-entry to the music business came via bassist Bill Laswell, who hired Baker to play on PiL's 1985 album, *Album*. Baker followed with his own *Horses & Trees* (which was mostly recorded to drum machine), *Ginger Baker's African Force*, and *Middle Passage*, the latter two combining Western and African music. He joined the Black Sabbath–inspired trio Masters of Reality for a recording in '93. In 1994 Baker returned to his jazz roots on *Going Back Home*, which featured bassist Charlie Haden and guitarist Bill Frisell. *Falling Off the Roof* and *Coward of the County* followed in a similar vein.

Baker retuned to Africa in the '90s and was not heard from again until the massively successful Cream reunion of 2005, which resulted in a tour and popular DVD.

GEAR & SETUP

Ginger Baker designed and built his first drum set from Perspex, or acrylic, bent and shaped on his parent's gas stove. He played this kit on his early gigs until purchasing a secondhand professional kit when he was 17, though he continued to use his Perspex set until Jack Bruce trashed it. The bass and snare drum were by Ludwig, the toms from the UK's top drum company, Premier. Ginger bought a new Ludwig set between late '65 and mid '66, not long before he joined Cream. His original Cream kit (assembled by London's Drum City) included two bass drums measuring 11×20 (right) and 11×22 (left), 8×12 and 9×13 mounted toms, 14×14 and 16×16 floor toms, and his long-suffering 1940s-era 6.5×14 Leedy wood snare drum. His Zildjian cymbal complement was sparse by today's standards: 15" hi-hats, 22" crash/ride, and 18" and 20" crashes to the left and right sides of the kit.

Ginger's cymbal setup changed slightly in 1967, no doubt in response to Cream's blast-furnace stage volume and increasing propensity for extended improvisations. The 15" hi-hats remained, augmented by 14", 18", 16", and 20" crashes, 20" ride and 22" crash-ride with rivets (with washers under the rivets), 8" splash, and cowbell. He also replaced the 11×22 bass drum with a standard 14×22.

Though some have suggested that Baker used Rogers hardware with Cream, this is in dispute, as some archival pictures definitely show Ludwig mounts and stands. During Cream's final tour Ginger did switch to a Ludwig 5.5×14 Supraphonic chrome snare drum, customized with a raised batter head to enable rim shots. He used Ludwig Fleetfoot pedals with leather straps (which would soon be replaced in the Ludwig line by the ubiquitous Speed King all-metal bass drum pedal).

By the early '90s Baker had piled on the cymbals while maintaining his by-now standard drum complement. His K Zildjian cymbal setup included 16" K Dark crash, 1966-era 14" hi-hats, 13" flat ride, 8" splash, 8" and 10" EFX, 1966-era 22" medium ride with rivets, 20" China, and an 18" medium ride.

His Ludwig kit now included a 5×14 copper snare and two 16×20 bass drums. Baker used Ludwig Ensemble series (coated) heads on snare, Silver Dots on all other drums.

At Cream's 2005 reunion gig at Albert Hall, Ginger played his traditional four-toms/double-bass-drum kit (though he had switched to Drum Workshop brand drums and heads), augmented with a plethora of tiny splash cymbals.

STYLE & TECHNIQUE

Ginger Baker's strengths were many, his interests varied, and his abilities as broad as the cosmos. His myriad, multi-tiered approach makes for a deep dish of drumming technique to explore and learn from.

In his day, Baker took drumming further out than anyone before him, practically inventing the expressive drum language we now take for granted. Before Baker, rock drummers largely played it straight, breaking out occasionally but never stamping the music with an identifiable personality. Even today, Baker's choice of sources and notes sounds inspired and wonderfully odd. What he played is no big deal by today's technical standards, but it retains an air of majesty, magic, and mystery. Sure, you can easily trace the connection between his trad jazz leanings and his cathartic solo outpourings, but considering his innovative pop drum parts—the backward beat in "Sunshine of Your Love," the colliding, Vinnie Colaiuta–like double-bass-drum concussion in the closing bars of "Strange Brew," and the kinetic "fla-doomp, fla-doomp, fla-doomp, fla-doomp, flap!" one-bar break in "Swlabr"—Baker was an inspired player whose work was overshadowed by drummers who favored bombast over rhythmic subtlety. Before Baker, drums were in the background; he opened the door through which every rock drummer from Bonham to Bozzio to Virgil Donati found his role.

Cream's first album, *Fresh Cream*, offers several examples of Baker's titanic, take-no-prisoners technique. The off-kilter tom introduction of "N.S.U." is followed by enormous, around-the-set single-stroke rolls, a seemingly backwards beat (with the accent on *one* and *three*, not *two* and *four*) in the second verse, and ruptured tom bashing as the trio wails in the song's closing moments. Like any good jazz drummer, Baker always followed the melody wherever it might lead. Slightly behind the beat, but with a smackdown approach that could change the direction of a song in a second, Baker shaped Cream with a subtle iron fist. Baker's psychotic cymbal bashing in "Cat's Squirrel" is matched by the boiling two-step rhythm of "Rollin' and Tumblin,'" where he follows Bruce's harmonica melody to its very end, dropping bombs and smashing his hi-hat in call and response.

Disraeli Gears featured Cream's first true hits, including "Sunshine of Your Love" (with Baker's famously backwards beat), "Tales of Brave Ulysses"

(Baker dropping regal tom fills and a bony, bucking groove), and "Swlabr," a fast tune with another fantastic, time-tumbling beat, flam accents, and memorable one-bar drum break.

Wheels of Fire was a watershed album for Baker, from his bolero-inspired 5/4 opening in "White Room" (for which he was not properly credited) and its tumbling, broken-time feel, to the slapping snare and grueling groove of "Politician," where Baker combines the low-down thud of jazz pioneer Baby Dodds with the heavy-metal thwack of Black Sabbath's Bill Ward. He performs a similar feat at a quicker tempo on "Born Under a Bad Sign." Ginger's snare-drum chops and expressive groove are further highlighted on the Arabic-tinged "Deserted Cities of the Heart"; a brisk single-stroke snare-drum figure flying over lush strings in the song's segue.

Baker will forever be known for "Toad"—the first rock drum solo— which can be heard in two incarnations: the studio version on *Fresh Cream*, and live on *Wheels of Fire*. The studio "Toad" again finds Baker matching Clapton's guitar melody before breaking off into dynamic tom-tom flam plunges and powerful 16th-note phrasings. He sets up the solo with a brief accented snare cadence, breaking it up with intertwined double-bass-drum drops and swing triplet tom variations, slowly incorporating all the toms, and leading to disjointed snare/bass drum combinations. He fumbles though some full-set triplets and single-stroke rolls between the two bass drums, adding subtle snare-drum ghost-notes, all over a driving eighth-note pulse. Baker then turns a corner, breaking into a jazz ride pattern, adding a bass-drum melody and hi-hat variations off the main time, of course. He slowly builds the interaction of the entire set into a tremendous wall of sound, the drums accenting en masse into a thudding, rolling tidal wave of rhythm. He incomprehensibly lays snare rolls underneath this storm of sand, then jabs the snare even harder, finally rolling the entire set in a full triplet display and a quick snare/cymbal climax before returning to the head with Clapton and Bruce.

Baker used both matched and traditional grips, befitting his combination of rock and jazz styles. More unusual was his flatly positioned double-mounted toms, which enabled a harder *thwack!* of rim shots as needed. Baker sat rather high to his low-leveled Leedy snare, again, giving him more power when needed.

Baker displayed full mastery of paradiddles, flams, ratamacues, and ruffs at will in various songs. The flam and the triplet were nonetheless his main weapons, along with single-stroke rolls. It was all couched in a subtly African approach to playing his tom-toms (both tonally and rhythmically) and which also seemed to influence their tuning. Baker preferred a dry thud on his toms and a whipsaw crack on his snare. He revved up the volume and crunch for Cream but expressed his love of African rhythms in later bands like Air Force and the Baker-Gurvitz Army Band.

Also of note is Baker's fluid, flexible hi-hat work, a staple of his drumming that gave all his rhythms a slippery, evocative feel. He could also drop the hi-hat (via his foot pedal) into a rhythm while directing the song on the ride cymbal.

Consistently following the melody as would a jazz drummer, but supplying a massive groove underneath, Ginger Baker is the seminal musician who kicked rock drumming into the 20th century.

LESSON

To play like Ginger Baker, one must understand the power of rock and the complexity of jazz, and develop the ability and good taste to combine the two without letting the former overwhelm the latter. Baker often sounded clumsy out of context, his flamming tom fills flop-flop-flopping across an otherwise well-manicured Cream blues rock tune, but his chunky approach belied his extremely graceful and subtle skills. Executing lithesome jazz ride-cymbal patterns that lent his entire drum-set feel a loping, swinging style, Baker knew how to pour on the gas and charge through powerhouse blues-rock improvisations that were completely innovative in the innocent mid '60s. Baker style requirements include a working knowledge of trad jazz and stomping blues shuffles, rudimental snare-drum technique, and a touch of the mad genius.

Essentials

▶ Jazz ride cymbal patterns
▶ Rock grooves played with a jazz pulse
▶ Swing, shuffle, eighth-note rock, and 3/4 waltz patterns
▶ Full-set studies incorporating single-stroke rolls, flams, and ruffs
▶ Complete rudimental snare studies

Example 1

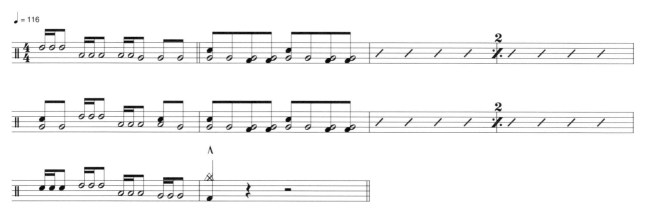

This pounding "Sunshine of Your Love"–style beat relies on a succession of eighth-notes played on the floor tom—"riding the floor tom" is the operative motion, coupled with Baker's trademark 16th-note descending tom fills. Imagine you are matching the low-end growl of a rubbery electric-bass line, topping off the basic beat with a fanfare of tom fills. Of special interest, and which may take some practice, is the snare accent falling on *one* and *three* rather than the typical *two* and *four*. The prominent *one/three* smack-down gives the beat a distinctively staccato attack.

Example 2

A master of the slippery beat, Baker's loosely played R&B-derived beats have a skipping quality, even if the actual notation here looks pretty straight. Baker plays the hi-hat even more loosely than is heard on this "White Room"–inspired beat, but focus on the beat's sprightly cadence, and think about the swooshing hi-hat sound (achieved by adjusting foot control pressure) after mastering the snare/bass-drum beat.

Example 3

A classic loping Baker pattern—think "Politician"—driven here by a briskly bouncing shuffle-oriented right-hand cymbal pattern and unusually popping snare-drum accents. The quarter-note snare accents loosely follow the guitar and bass lines, giving the entire song a lumbering, giraffe-like feel.

Example 4

Another example of Baker's fanfare-oriented tom fill style, similar to "Sunshine of Your Love" but with even grander groove and flow, à la "Badge." The 16th-note tom fills (a Baker staple) are larger in attitude and slightly slower, and the floor tom is ridden with an even more majestic sense of purpose. Imagine you are entering the gates of some medieval city, riding your steed to a martial pulse.

CHAPTER 2
John Bonham

It is no exaggeration to say that John Henry Bonham ushered in a revolution in drumming that can be felt to this day. In *his* day, Bonham was considered simply the greatest rock 'n' roll drummer alive, and for many that description still holds true. But Bonham's thunderous sound and blistering technical facility have a much broader influence than the classic rockers of Led Zeppelin could have ever imagined.

John Bonham's drumming is the foundation of rock and heavy-metal drumming, and, most recently, the hip-hop world of loops and sampled effects. Sure, every drummer old enough to grip a pair of sticks still sees John Bonham, aka Bonzo, as the be-all and end-all of modern rock drumming, but his titanic thud-like consistency has also become the standard for the rock and hip-hop drum loop. In an age when any drummer's essential beats can be sampled, spliced, and looped for a producer's needs, Bonham's incredibly pure drum tone and equally powerful technical assault is the ideal for modern drum production. While it is impossible to know with certainty which producers and artists have literally sampled Bonzo's wicked beats, his feel can be heard in everything from the crunch of Dr. Dre and Nas to the bombast of Korn and Trent Reznor's Nine Inch Nails.

BIOGRAPHY

Born on May 31, 1948, to a working-class family in Redditch, England, John Henry Bonham started banging on pots and pans, bath-salts containers, and coffee cans to accompany his already boisterous personality when he was only five. His mother bought him his first snare drum when he was 10, and by 15 he had a full-sized secondhand Premier drum set. Inspired by Gene Krupa's role in 1955's *The Benny Goodman Story*, the young Bonham realized that drummers could be more than timekeepers, that they could steal the show. Buddy Rich was another early hero. Bonham found a local teacher who exposed him to the Humphrey Lyttleton jazz band, whose drummer pounded out a floor-tom solo using only his hands. Later, Bonham would fall for the extended jazz solos of the pre-Cream Ginger Baker, then with the Graham Bond Organisation.

Though Redditch was not a hub of musical activity, Bonham played with a series of proto rock 'n' roll bands, including A Way of Life, the Senators, and the aptly named Locomotive. Even then Bonham's ego pushed the music to extremes, the drummer often lining his bass drum with tin foil so the *boom!* would project even more. It was then that Bonham crossed paths with future Led Zeppelin lead singer Robert Plant, who in 1967 asked the drummer to join his group Band of Joy. The band recorded several demos but no record contract materialized. The band soon bombed, and the pair went their separate ways until early 1968 when, with word of Bonham's titanic groove and volume (and overbearing personality) reaching London, he was asked by guitarist and session ace Jimmy Page (who has already enlisted Plant) to join the re-formed Yardbirds, then the hottest British R&B band in England. After a sarcastic Keith Moon suggested that the band's first gig would "go over like a lead zeppelin," they quickly changed their name and entered the annals of classic rock history.

From their 1969 debut, *Led Zeppelin*, to their final 1979 release, *In Through the Out Door*, Bonham reinvented the standard rock beat, just as the band stretched rock's borders and boundaries. Bonham's heavy yet dexterous bass drum patterns raised the standard for what was once considered a four-to-the-bar timepiece, his single bass drum often mirroring a mammoth double-bass-drum approach. Accompanied by bassist John Paul Jones, Bonham created volcanic bedrock that was without equal. And though Bonham's reputation as a full-scale hell raiser preceded him, his intake of alcohol never impaired his drumming. Bonham's swinging anchor of a beat took hold in *Led Zeppelin*'s "Dazed and Confused" and "Communication Breakdown." *Led*

Zeppelin II featured the global hit "Whole Lotta Love" and Bonham's roundhouse tom-tom rolls, which enter the song like a battalion of Nazi warplanes. Starting the fill with an accent on the last 16th before the downbeat of *one*, then continuing the actual roll on the 16th before *two*, Bonham instantly grabs your attention and propels the song forward. Bonham's stampeding pummel fills *Led Zeppelin III*'s "Immigrant Song," while *Led Zeppelin IV* features four landmark Bonham grooves: the time-inverted kick-in-the-head stomp of "Black Dog," the bashing hi-hat and 4/4 assault of "Rock and Roll," the epic chug of "Stairway to Heaven," and the ultimate slow-motion beat of doom, "When the Levee Breaks." Bonham plays funk with a malevolent glee on *Houses of the Holy*'s "The Crunge," displays his mighty bass-drum technique and sense of space on *Physical Graffiti*'s classic "Kashmir," and elicits swinging triplet-based funk and Latin bell patterns on *In Through the Out Door*'s "Fool in the Rain."

Even though tales of debauchery dogged Led Zeppelin's tours, the group continued to sell millions of records. But the partying took its toll. A family man at heart who hated flying, post performance Bonham would often drink most

CHECKLIST ✓

❏ Drums
1970s Ludwig Vistalite

❏ Condition
New, orange and blue

❏ Sticks
Ludwig 2A

❏ Setup
Sits even with snare drum, legs at 90-degree angle

❏ Effects
Tympani, maracas, tambourine, Ludwig cowbell (made by Paiste), Paiste 38" symphonic gong, congas

❏ Feel
Massive, titanic, doom-laden; slightly behind the beat but aggressive

❏ Signature traits
Slamming bass-drum execution, volcanic groove, funky beat, time inversion, maniacal cymbal smashes

❏ Influences
Big band, '50s jazz, early rock 'n' roll

❏ Overall approach
Titanically sludgy groove matched by cacophonous tom fills, flurry of single-stroke rolls, inventive tom fills, and thunderous energy; a rock drummer playing with the impact and power of 20 big-band drummers

SELECTED DISCOGRAPHY

With Led Zeppelin:

Led Zeppelin
Led Zeppelin II
Led Zeppelin III
Led Zeppelin IV
Houses of the Holy
Physical Graffiti
Presence
In Through the Out Door
How the West Was Won

RECOMMENDED CUTS

"Moby Dick" (*Led Zeppelin II*)
"Kashmir" (*Physical Graffiti*)
"The Crunge" (*Houses of the Holy*)
"Black Dog" (*Led Zeppelin IV*)
"Rock and Roll" (*Led Zeppelin IV*)
"Misty Mountain Hop" (*Led Zeppelin IV*)
"Whole Lotta Love" (*Led Zeppelin II*)
"When the Levee Breaks" (*Led Zeppelin IV*)
"The Ocean" (*Houses of the Holy*)
"Achilles Last Stand" (*Presence*)

everyone under the table, then proceed to destroy hotel rooms in true rock 'n' roll fashion. One such drinking binge occurred on September 24, 1980. The band was to begin rehearsals at Bray Studios for an upcoming U.S. tour, Zeppelin's first since 1977. En route to the studio Bonham drank four quadruple vodkas and, on arriving, continued his drinking. Later that evening the band retired to Jimmy Page's house in Windsor. Bonham fell asleep and was put to bed by a roadie. He was found dead the next morning, the cause of death cited as "asphyxiation caused by choking on his own vomit." John Bonham was buried on October 10, 1980, at Rushock parish churchyard, near the Old Hyde farm.

GEAR & SETUP

Bonham's trademark Vistalite drums have become an icon of sorts, the drummer once called "the Beast" experiencing such eternal popularity that Ludwig recently reissued the Vistalite line for today's heavy-metal timekeepers. Bonham played both blue and orange Vistalites, complemented by a massive (for that era) 14×26 bass drum, 10×14 mounted tom, and 16×16 and 16×18 floor toms, as well as an all-metal Supraphonic 402 6.5×14 snare drum with 42-strand snares.

Bonham always played Paiste cymbals, beginning with the Giant Beat series; he then switched to the Sound Edge line, his complement of 15" hi-hats, 18" medium crash, 24" ride, and 20" medium crash rather minimal by today's more-is-better 'n' bigger standards. (Though his setup would change and expand though the years.)

Bonham was a traditionalist in many ways, such as his choice of Remo Coated Emperor heads. For his bass drum Bonham preferred an Emperor Coated batter with a Medium Coated on the resonant side with felt strips on both heads. His rack and floor toms were outfitted with an Emperor coated top and Ambassador Coated bottom, while his snare drum sported an Emperor Coated batter side with an Ambassador or a Diplomat on the bottom. His bass drum pedal was the then-ubiquitous Ludwig

Speed King. Though he was a traditionalist in his choice of heads, Bonham's tuning was unusual: Instead of the normal practice of tuning both heads to similar pitches, he preferred his bottom head much tighter than the top.

Drum tech Jeff Ocheltree worked in the studio with Bonham in 1977 and '79. Here, he describes Bonzo's tuning to Drummerworld.com: "John tuned his drums like many drummers who played large drums in the big band era, in that the bass drum heads were pitched a lot higher than one would think. The reason for that was he was moving a lot of air, and the impact of the beater on the head—you want air to move quickly to get a round full sound."

Ocheltree also noted that this tighter-than-usual tuning resulted in Bonzo's signature sound. In particular, his bottom tom heads were tighter than the batter side, almost as tight as a snare drum head. Similarly, Bonzo pitched the snare side of the snare drum higher than the batter though without choking the snares. The top head on the snare was also tight, but always with an ear to maintaining dynamic levels between the two heads.

Bonham's Ludwig kits evolved through the years. His first Ludwig endorsement kit, enabled by Carmine Appice in 1969, was finished in Natural Maple Thermo-gloss. He played his third and perhaps most popular kit, his Ludwig Amber Vistalites, on Led Zeppelin's U.S. tour in 1973. The dimensions were as follows: 6.5×14 Chrome Supra-Phonic Snare Drum with Gretsch 42-strand power snares, 10×14 tom, 16×16 and 16×18 floor toms, 14×26 bass drum with cymbal mount, and 29" and 30" Ludwig Machine Timpani Drums. His fourth and final kit was a massive stainless steel set with a massive 12×15 mounted tom.

Bonzo's hardware included Rogers Swivo-matic cymbal stands, Rogers Swivo-matic hi-hat stands, and Ludwig Atlas snare stands and Ludwig Speed King bass drum pedals on all his kits. And a Ludwig Ching Ring on "Moby Dick."

STYLE & TECHNIQUE

Though Bonham is often described as a monster rampaging through Led Zeppelin like a bull in a china shop, he was actually a very sensitive drummer. Rather than pound his drums, Bonham knew how to draw the sound from them. His touch was comparatively light by today's metal standards, and Bonham's technique was thoroughly grounded in jazz and big band music. The opening bars of the live version of "Moby Dick," knowingly or not, reference Max Roach's classic ¾ drum solo "The Drum Also Waltzes" before Bonham gives a lesson in rudimental proficiency that covers crossovers, snare-to-tom paradiddles, full-set triplets, blazing snare and bass-drum patterns, and lightning fast, impossibly smooth single-stroke rolls. That speed extended to his powerful full-set triplets, which when combined with an excellent sense of dynamics, gave Bonham incredible soloing prowess—not to mention his use of hands on the heads, which added further dimensions, both visual and sonic, to his drumming arsenal. Add to that his signature loping funk patterns and Goliath sonic imprint, and you have one of the greatest drum stylists of all time.

Perhaps more interesting than his splendid solo technique (which often resulted in 30-minute-plus improvisations) were the revolutionary patterns Bonham created for such memorable tracks as "Kashmir," "Whole Lotta Love," "Fool in the Rain," "The Crunge," and "Black Dog." The latter is a textbook example of Bonham's practice of inverting a 4/4 measure to create an off-kilter feeling, then resolving the time before the listener realizes what has happened. Doubling Jimmy Page's floating guitar riff, Bonham plays a single-stroke roll on the snare beginning on the second 16th of *two*, leading to a *three*-"and" accent on the bass drum and a hard *four* on the snare before playing the bass drum on the first beat of the verse, finally creating a sense of stability. After a brief bar of straight time, Bonham then plays a double-16th on the bass drum into *one* on the snare and a heavy crash on the following "and" of *one*. He repeats this three times separated by rubato vocal passages, finally extending the groove with a thunderous Latin bell/tom figure in the chorus. Later in the song Bonham will accent the last 16th before and the eighth after the downbeat of the verse pattern to further syncopate the time, Bonzo-style. Throughout, he plays muscular snare/tom flams, slamming full-set triplets, and even some smooth grace notes. Listen carefully in the rests and you can hear Bonham clicking the sticks to cue his bandmates. It's not impossible once you count it out (similar to the call-to-war groove of "Rock and Roll"), but some 30 years after its release, Bonham's time tumbling performance on "Black Dog" still thrills.

LESSON

To play like John Bonham, weight-lifting might help, for starters. But even with his extreme power, Bonham was surprisingly graceful. Archival Led Zeppelin videos show him playing high off the drum kit, executing flashy big-band-derived fills that include full-set triplets, swinging cymbal patterns, and titanic tom rolls, all executed within a Hindenburg-like time feel (often based in an odd meter). Bonham style requirements include full knowledge of swing triplets, speed, odd meters, rudimental snare-drum prowess, and a broad reach around the set.

Essentials
- ▶ Tom rolls based on swing triplets
- ▶ Cymbal patterns (some irregular) based on Afro-Cuban and swing
- ▶ Odd meters played with a rock pulse
- ▶ Swing, shuffle, twist, and 3/4 waltz patterns
- ▶ Rhythmic groups that begin after the downbeat

Example 1

A mammoth drum sound, nimble cowbell rhythm, and quick doubled 16th-note-triplet bass-drum kicks comprise the bulk of this classic Bonham beat inspired by "Good Times Bad Times." Performed slightly ahead of the beat but with a dragging feel on the cowbell, the message is basically slamming *two* and *four,* but the unusual bass-drum kicks require practice. The opening snare/tom accents mirror the bass and guitar intro. To familiarize your limbs with these fast strokes, practice a 16th-note Brazilian samba pattern: uh-*one,* uh-*two,* uh-*three,* uh-*four* (where the 16th-note count is *one* -e-and-uh, *two* -e-and-uh, etc). Also note the intro hi-hat pulse, which progresses from 1 and 3 to straight 4, and the flashy single-stroke roll into the body of the groove.

Example 2

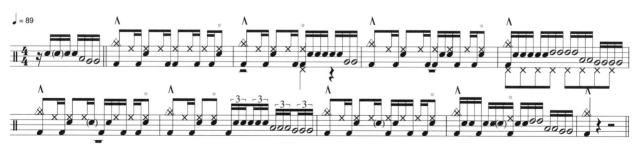

A perfect example of Bonham's forward-motion Goliath, this "Whole Lotta Love"–style beat is super-syncopated, with a slippery, seriously funky hi-hat pattern. Bonham's round-the-kit tom roll gives the song a tremendous feeling of lift and feels like you are diving off a cliff. The entire pattern—snare, bass drum, and toms—replicates Jimmy Page's storming guitar riff, especially the snare accent on the "an" of *four* of every other bar. Note how the opening snare/tom roll anticipates the downbeat of the first bar. And if you can manage the 16th-note triplets, go for it!

Example 3

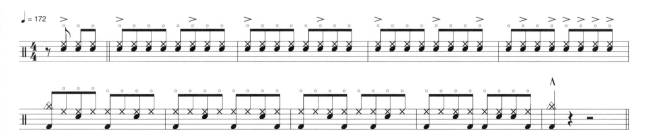

The snare/hi-hat accents that kick off the "Rock and Roll"–styled beat actually begin before the downbeat of the bar, and in a very tricky 16th-note segment. Try to replicate the snare/hi-hat intro as closely as possible, perhaps even setting the track on repeat and playing it as a loop until you grasp its unusual count-in. Reading the music is imperative. After that freaky intro, it's pretty much a simple *two* and *four* on the snare and *one* and *three* on the bass drum.

Example 4

This cut-time, slower version of the beat gives greater insight into Bonham's unique ability to make a difficult beat sound deceptively simple—if you do the work, that is! And don't forget to flow.

Example 5

Track 9

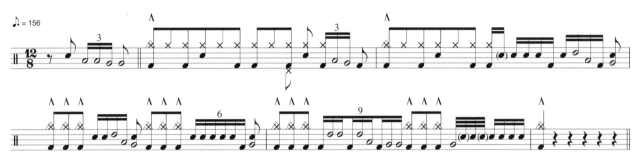

A slow 6/8 blues pattern highlighted by massive tom fills and—in the feet of our CD drummer Donnie Marshall—killer bass drum/tom roll combinations. As with the "Whole Lotta Love" pattern, this "Dazed and Confused" beat follows the guitar line, augmented by a combination of 16th- and eighth-note triplets and big quarter-note cymbal/bass-drum accents.

CHAPTER 3
Stewart Copeland

Stewart Copeland was one of the most exciting and influential of all '80s rock drummers. Like the Eveready bunny smashing together rock, reggae, and punk, Copeland moved his long, gangly limbs in perpetual motion on such Police million-sellers as "Message in a Bottle," "Can't Stand Losing You," "Every Little Thing She Does Is Magic," and "Roxanne." Copeland's trademark rhythmic inventions have been absorbed into the drum-set lexicon by drummers as diverse as Danny Carey (Tool) and Taylor Hawkins (Foo Fighters), who replicate his hyper rim figures, galvanic offbeat fills, Latin bell patterns, whipsaw hi-hat figures, tumbling Octoban explosions, flam patterns, and blazing single-stroke rolls, all of which helped seal Copeland's manic energy deal. Of course, Copeland's ahead-of-the-beat time feel and frenetic demeanor are the twin ingredients that helped spell the demise of The Police, but without his resourcefulness and drive, the English trio (including Sting and Andy

Summers) might have faded into history along with the punk and New Wave scene from which they sprouted.

BIOGRAPHY

Born on July 16, 1952, in Alexandria, Egypt, Copeland—the son of a CIA agent—attended boarding school in Lebanon and college in California before relocating to England and entering its vibrant music scene in 1975. He soon landed a gig with progressive rock unit Curved Air, with whom he recorded two albums, *Midnight Wire* and *Airborne*. Following that group's conclusion and inspired by the nascent English punk scene, Copeland formed The Police with singer/bassist Sting and guitarist Henri Padovani (who, after a brief stint with the band, was replaced by the jazz-leaning Andy Summers). Beginning with their first album, 1978's *Outlandos D'Amours*, The Police became a global phenomenon, drawing from rock, punk, and Caribbean folk music to create a uniquely catchy and unusually intellectual pop sound that produced such worldwide smash singles as "Every Breath You Take," "De Do Do Do, De Da Da Da," "King of Pain," and "Don't Stand So Close to Me." Not to be outdone, Copeland issued his first solo record in 1980, *Music Madness from the Kinetic Kid*, under the alias Klark Kent.

Copeland received critical and popular acclaim for his innovative drumming with The Police, and he contributed songs (and occasionally vocals) to the trio's long run of hit albums. As important to the group's sound as Sting's vocals or Summers's guitar, Copeland's drumming was the rhythmic juggernaut that both propelled and grounded each song, from his ricocheting, dub-heavy snare-drum rhythms in "The Bed's Too Big Without You" and the feathery hi-hat patterns of "Every Little Thing She Does Is Magic" to the indecipherable (and multitracked) rim fusillades of "Reggatta De Blanc" and the time-twisting, *three*-centric feel of "Walking on the Moon." And don't miss the manic beauty of Copeland's marvelously speed-ridden single-stroke rolls and flam-laden, triplet-framed four-bar exchanges in "No Time This Time." Copeland could also groove like nobody's business, as in pocket-heavy ravers like "Shambelle," "Flexible Strategies," "Murder by Numbers," and "Demolition Man." Live, Copeland's energetic time feel pushed the band to the edge of madness, as can be seen in Copeland's 2006 DVD *Everyone Stares: The Police Inside Out*, where, in one scene, Summers glares at the drummer and mouths the words: "Too fast!" Yet it was that forward motion, coupled with Copeland's unique rhythmic concepts and blazing technique, that provided the basis of The Police's musical innovations and popularity.

Copeland also contributed a handful of songs to The Police canon. His compositions expressed the left-of-center, oddball focus that would surface in a series of highly original solo albums such as *The Rhythmatist*, as well as early film scores like *Talk Radio*. Along with Summers—whose compositional acumen in songs like "Someone to Talk To" paled next to the mighty Sting pen—Copeland wrote the first Police single, the punk blowtorch "Fallout," and plodding nursery rhyme "On Any Other Day," as well as virtual throwaways like "Bombs Away," "Miss Grandenko," and "A Sermon." But Copeland also composed a handful of gems, as in the beautifully brooding midnight epic "Darkness" from *Ghost in the Machine.*

The Police disbanded after their 1983 tour, freeing Copeland to work on his burgeoning career as a film composer. (He earned a Golden Globe nomination for the score to Francis Ford Coppola's *Rumble Fish.*) In 1985 Copeland recorded *The Rhythmatist,* the product of his musical journey (both literally and figuratively) to Australia, the Congo, Easter Island, Mozambique, and the Caribbean. The percolating album featured traditional percussion and drum set as well as sampled car horns and noisily ticking clocks. Copeland continued to work in Hollywood, scoring a pair of Oliver Stone features, *Wall Street* and *Talk Radio,* in addition to such indie films as *Raining Stones, Four Days in September, West Beirut* and a handful of mainstream TV productions (most recently, an episode of *Desperate Housewives*). Copeland was the recipient of the Hollywood Film Festival's first Outstanding Music in Film Visionary Award.

After The Police imploded, Copeland played with a variety of artists, appearing on Peter Gabriel's *So,* with pop-fusion trio Animal Logic, on Stanley Clarke's *If This Bass Could Only Talk,* Strontium 90's *Police Academy,* and, in 2001, a trio of albums: Oysterhead's *Grand Pecking Order* (with members of Phish and Primus), The Racketeers' *Mad for the Racket,* and Tom Waits's *Alice.* Even with the restraints of production budgets and other artist's needs, Copeland's trademark creativity was still in evidence. Concurrent with those projects, Copeland also composed such symphonic works as *King Lear* for the San Francisco Ballet, *Holy Blood and Crescent Moon* for the Cleveland Opera, and *Prey* for Ballet Oklahoma.

Though The Police eventually re-formed for a world tour in early 2007, Copeland continued to pursue soundtrack work and solo projects, most recently including *Orchestralli,* a 2005 CD/DVD featuring Copeland on drums accompanied by a small orchestral ensemble and a four-piece percussion quartet. Additionally, his yearly Italian touring supergroup, Gizmo!, performs many of Copeland's compositions, past and present, and a few Police numbers. Copeland's career includes the sale of more than 40 million records worldwide, and he has won five Grammy Awards.

GEAR & SETUP

Stewart Copeland's drum set has evolved since the late '70s, but two things remain constant: Tama drums and Paiste cymbals (though he has acknowledged using a Ludwig chrome snare on many Police hit singles). By the early '80s Copeland's nine-ply Midnight Blue Tama Imperial Star setup had solidified to include a 14×22 bass drum (triggering a Synare electronic pad), 5×14 snare drum, 8×10, 8×12, and 9×13 mounted toms, 16×16 floor tom, and two additional 8×12 and 9×13 mounted toms (on his left-hand side) with a single Roto-tom over his hi-hat. Four Tama Octobans augmented the drum setup. Woodblocks could sometimes be seen on the left side of his kit.

Copeland's '80s-era Paiste cymbal complement comprised Formula 602 13" medium hi-hats, a 16" thin crash, two 8" 2002 bell cymbals, two 8" and one 11" 2002 splashes, and RUDE 14", 16", and 22" crash-rides. His studio setup was similar and included Formula 2002 16" and 18" medium rides and a 22" 602 heavy ride. A percussion rack contained a Tama Gong bass, timbales, bongos, xylophone, tuned percussion, bells, gongs, and chimes.

The Tamas were mostly paired with Remo Weather King Coated Ambassador heads, with Remo Emperors on the tom batters and a CS Black Dot on the bass batter (with CS Black Dot

Copeland was an early fan of signal processing and effects, explaining his rig and approach to *Downbeat* in 1984, the year of The Police breakup:

"I tried double-bass drumming when I was with Curved Air, but...now I get the same effect with delays. So I've been using the delays for years and

CHECKLIST ✓

❏ Drums
Tama Stewart Copeland Signature and Paiste Signature cymbals

❏ Condition
New

❏ Sticks
Vater Stewart Copeland

❏ Setup
Sits even with snare drum, legs at 90-degree angle and slightly high off kit

❏ Effects
Minimal

❏ Feel
Ahead of the beat, loping, aggressive, *three-*centric, Afro-Cuban, Caribbean

❏ Signature traits
Feathery hi-hat work, blazing single-strokes, manic time feel, unique bell patterns, lightning-fast rim work

❏ Influence
Big band, Buddy Rich, Ginger Baker, '50s jazz, West Indian and Arabic music

❏ Overall approach
Extremely lithe and brisk feel matched by explosive single-stroke rolls, unexpected rim click flurries and "drop" tom patterns; a dancer on the drums

SELECTED DISCOGRAPHY

With The Police:

Outlandos D'Amours
Reggatta De Blanc
Zenyatta Mondatta
Ghost in the Machine
Synchronicity

With Oysterhead:

Grand Pecking Order

Solo albums:

The Rhythmatist
Orchestralli

RECOMMENDED CUTS

"No Time This Time" (*Reggatta de Blanc*)
"Roxanne" (*Outlandos d'Amour*)
"The Bed's Too Big Without You" (*Reggatta de Blanc*)
"Murder by Numbers" (*Synchronicity*)
"One World (Not Three)" (*Ghost in the Machine*)
"Tea in the Sahara" (*Synchronicity*)
"Reggatta de Blanc" (*Reggatta de Blanc*)
"Deathwish" (Reggatta de Blanc)
"It's Alright for You" (*Reggatta de Blanc*)
"Bring on the Night" (*Reggatta de Blanc*)
"Can't Stand Losing You" (*Outlandos d'Amour*)
"Message in a Bottle" (*Reggatta de Blanc*)

years, but I keep checking out the new ones. See, with longer delay times, you lose the high end; but now the chips are getting smarter so you can maintain the high end over longer delays."

In '84 Copeland was using state-of-the-art electronic delays, including Delta Lab, AMS, and Roland 2000 digital delays triggered by foot pedals placed next to his hi-hat. He also used Electro-Harmonix Instant Replay, which allowed him to record sounds, load them into a Simmons pad, then play them back almost instantly, quite a feat in those nascent days of electronic drum tweaking.

Copeland also outlined his stage accessories to *Downbeat*; they included a Yamaha HandySound HS-501 polyphonic mini-synth, a Casio PT20 monophonic mini-synth, a Boss Dr. Rhythm, the Scholz Rockman ("for studio effects"), a Fostex X-15 Multi-tracker cassette recorder, Sanyo C mini-monitor speakers, and Sony headphones, plus a Fender Stratocaster "for that dose of heavy metal."

Copeland's current setup with Gizmo! reflects his typically wide-ranging influences and his Paiste and Tama allegiances—but virtually no electronics. His Tama Stewart Copeland Signature model drums run, left to right: 5×14 SC145 Stewart Copeland Signature Palette snare drum, 10×13 floor tom, 9×10 and 10×12 toms, 16×16 and 16×18 floor toms, 18×22 bass drum. Paiste Signature cymbals follow, left to right: 13" Dark Crisp hi-hats, 8" Bell, 16" Fast Crash, 8", 10", and 12" Splashes, 18" Full Crash, 21" Dry Heavy Ride, 18" Fast Crash, 18" Light Flat Ride, and 16" Full Crash.

His Remo head complement: Remo Emperor clear batter and Remo Ambassador clear bottom for toms, Remo Ambassador Coated and Remo Ambassador Snare for the snare drum, Remo Powerstroke 4 Clears on the bass drum. Sticks are Vater Stewart Copeland Standard.

STYLE & TECHNIQUE

Blasting into London's punk scene with a history in psychedelic, Third World, and Arabic music, Copeland's technique was unusual, to say the least.

Playing with great finesse or power as the situation demanded and with the by-then-unused traditional grip, Copeland brought something to the table no one else had yet dreamed of: a focus on centering the pulse around *three* rather than *two* and *four*.

As he told *Modern Drummer* in 1982: "The backbeat has always done it in rock 'n' roll up to now, but the watershed in drumming, which West Indian music has brought about, means it's no longer so important. Alternatives have been discovered, such as bass drum four in the bar. Boom, boom, boom, boom. And instead of a backbeat on *two* and *four*, a rimshot on *three*."

Unable to play the drums as a teen in his Beirut boarding school, Copeland developed part of his cerebral approach by air-drumming his way through ideas and concepts. Again, from *Modern Drummer*:

"I found I was actually able to make lots of progress by thinking about drums as I walked along and I would just have drums in my mind. Not just drums, but rhythm, and I'd think in rhythm. In fact, I'd conceptualize in rhythm and form word patterns in rhythm. I would find that after a whole week of not actually playing the drums, when I'd go back to them I had made real progress. Not necessarily playing the things I thought of, but I would just find that my hands were working more smoothly and I could get that feeling more easily."

Regarding his current technique, Copeland told this writer (for a 2006 *Modern Drummer* piece): "The only consideration I ever give to technique is when I am warming up for a tour. Every summer I go to Italy, and a month or two before that I start warming up using technique: single-stroke rolls, paradiddles, all that kind of stuff. I am very disciplined about starting off every day's exercise with all of that technique stuff. Then when I put some CDs on with the earphones and jam along and start having fun, everything works better. I have learned over the decades of playing that the more correct the warm-up is, the better you can play. And it is really worth applying the discipline. It is sort of like a Zen, a hand yoga or something like that. It is deeply engrossing—it is kind of a meditation to get into those exercises. And then once they are done the reward is how well the hands work."

"Message in a Bottle" is an exceptional example of Copeland's technique. Beginning with an eighth-note flam pattern on the snare drum and a call-and response bass drum in the intro, Copeland breaks into a *three*-centric pulse for the verse (accenting the *three* on the bass drum). He charges into a straight *two*-and-*four* feel for the bridge, soon opening it up with "drop" tom accents on "3 an", accentuating the last 16th-note of the beat with a brisk snare fill and splash crash before the downbeat of the four-to-the-bar bass-drum-driven verse section (Sting singing "message in a bottle, yeah"). The verse bar repeats, Copeland playing sparse tom drops. The second verse is different from the first and similar to the intro, but with Copeland playing a four-to-the-bar bass drum accompanied only by an eighth-note high-hat pattern and tom accents on *three*-"and." This was revolutionary stuff for '80s pop radio. And Copeland's innovations are on full display: supercharged flams, rapid-fire rim click patterns, deft splashes, a *three*-centric beat, manic bell accents, off-kilter tom fills, and very fast hands.

LESSON

To play like Stewart Copeland one must be familiar with music of many cultures. Of course, the world is smaller today than in the late '70s, with practically every kind of world music (a term not known then) available on CD or from download. Just consider the wealth of styles Copeland employs, with stellar drumming throughout: punk, rock, reggae, Arabic, Caribbean, symphonic, rudimental. A cross-section of Copeland classics addresses punk ("Truth Hits Everybody"), reggae ("One World"), dub ("Bed's Too Big Without You"), and Latin ("Roxanne"). Copeland style requirements include knowledge of these differing types of music along with exceptional snare-drum technique, Latin bell patterns, flams (flamadiddles, drag flams, flam taps), full-set fluidity, and frenetic energy.

Essentials

▶ Rudimental studies focusing on single-stroke rolls and flams
▶ Afro-Cuban cymbal bell patterns
▶ 3/4 meter mastery
▶ 4/4 grooves with an emphasis on reggae and the *three* pulse or t*hree* drop
▶ Flam patterns played both on drums and between rim and drum
▶ Speed!
▶ Rudimental studies replicated on hi-hat

Example 1

What makes this unique "Roxanne"-style beat so distinctive is its delicate hi-hat trills and rhythmic pushing of the time, which give the rather standard bass and snare patterns an extreme sense of forward motion. The bell pattern that follows the hi-hat accomplishes the same feat, and opens the beat up wide for the chorus.

Example 2

A study in slow-motion reggae drama—check out "Walking on the Moon"—this beat also benefits from exacting hi-hat figures (as above) and is further heightened by the dramatic bass-drum bombs on *two*, and rim click drops on *three* (which are syncopated after the original *one-three* announcement). Practice embellishment sticking (drags, rolls, ruffs) on the hi-hat with the bass drum on *two* and *four*, then work in the rim click on *three*. Slow and easy does it.

Example 3

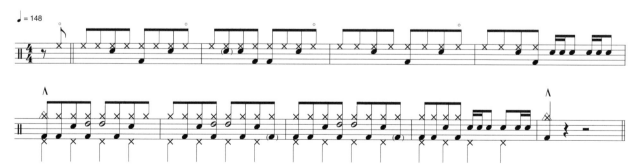

If you remove the cymbals and the bass drum downbeat from this ska-inspired "Message in a Bottle"–type rhythm, you have a fairly standard rock groove, and that may be the best way to "hear" it. As always, Copeland's tricky hi-hat embellishments require practice, their kinetic sparks pushing the beat around with a slippery grace. Copeland revs up the beat in the chorus (after the first four bars), doubling bass-drum accents on "1 an" and dropping funky tom "ba-booms" on the "an 3" of the bar while a straight eighth-note ride cymbal pattern further opens up the groove. A rather brisk pace ratchets up the difficulty level of this powerfully driving groove.

Example 4

A driving four-to-the-bar bass drum underpins a series of expansive tom drops (replicating Copeland's Octaban fills) and ricocheting 16th-note hi-hat figures—just a few tools from Stewart Copeland's arsenal.

CHAPTER 4
Richie Hayward

As primary earth mover in Little Feat for 35-plus years, Richie Hayward has contoured the California band's unmistakable amalgam of blues, roots, funk, and fusion with a left-of-center but perpetually soulful approach that made him one of the most influential drummers of the 1970s. Hayward's original grooves, tremendous funk feeling, and inventive rhythmic patterns are confirmed in classic Little Feat tracks like "Dixie Chicken," "Day at the Dog Races," "Easy to Slip," "The Fan," and "Fat Man in the Bathtub." Hayward's creativity has stretched beyond Little Feat, his work appearing on recordings of Eric Clapton, Ry Cooder, the Doobie Brothers, Buddy Guy, Nils Lofgren, Taj Mahal, Robert Palmer, Van Dyke Parks, Robert Plant, Bob Seger, Carly Simon, Stephen Stills, Tom Waits, and Warren Zevon.

BIOGRAPHY

Born in Ames, Iowa, Hayward took an interest in the drums at age three when he saw a marching drummer in a local parade. His parents weren't crazy about his drumming aspirations, but they nonetheless purchased him a $150 set on which he bashed in their garage. Hayward would later join the school orchestra but found the discipline needed to learn classical music stifling. Playing with records proved more exciting, especially those with big-band drummers Jack Sperling, Sonny Payne, and bop pioneers Max Roach and Art Blakey. (His influences would later expand to include Mitch Mitchell, Philly Joe Jones, Manu Katché, Charlie Watts, and Zigaboo Modeliste.) Hayward played his first gig—standards at a Shriners' club—when he was 12; by high school he was already in a rock 'n' roll band playing local frat houses and roller rinks.

Hayward left Ames for Los Angeles in 1966 when he was 19 and rented a small apartment in Hollywood. Answering an ad in a free paper that was looking for a drummer who "must be freaky," Hayward met his future in songwriter/guitarist Lowell George, who was then playing in a group called the Factory. Two years later (after dabbling in political pop band Fraternity of Man), Hayward joined George in Little Feat, which included guitarist Paul Barrére, keyboardist Bill Payne, and bassist Kenny Gradney. Led by George and his beautiful, bizarre songwriting, the band was heavily influenced by the blues and R&B as well as such then-contemporary bands as Canned Heat, Frank Zappa's Mothers of Invention, and blues giant Howlin' Wolf. Hence, Little Feat's incorporation of both standard blues and rock 'n' roll and the more unconventional, anything-goes approach of the Mothers, of which George was occasionally a member. This melting-pot approach also affected Hayward, who was by now enjoying the Meters, Professor Longhair, and Clifton Chenier, which developed his drumming bent for New Orleans second-line rhythms. The caliber of Little Feat's diverse members made for music that could strike the Top 40 but which also developed a hardcore cult following.

A country-fried, blues-brawling, rock 'n' roll debut, 1971's *Little Feat* introduced the band to the public. *Sailin' Shoes* followed, with killer cuts like the almost–Top 40 hit "Easy to Slip," boogie-woogie bruiser "Teenage Nervous Breakdown," desert prowler "Cold Cold Cold," and George's classic storytelling ode to "weeds, whites and wine," "Willin'" Little Feat almost fired Hayward during the recording of 1973's *Dixie Chicken*, but he was fully re-ensconced by the time of '74's *Feats Don't Fail Me Now. The Last Record Album* announced, for all practical purposes, the end of Lowell George's songwriting control of Little Feat and the rise of the fusion influence heard on the following *Time Loves a Hero.* Though some fans decried this change in direction, for drummers the album is a gold mine of progressive grooves. Lowell George died during the recording of 1979's *Down on the Farm*, and Little Feat disbanded for seven years.

During this time and after a debilitating motorcycle accident, Hayward stayed busy recording with Joan Armatrading, Robert Plant, Nils Lofgren, Tom Waits, Warren Zevon, and Martha Velez. Even before Little Feat's breakup, Hayward had recorded with Ry Cooder, Barbra Streisand, Robert Palmer, Stephen Stills, Carly Simon, John Cale, and the Doobie Brothers. Little Feat re-formed for 1988's *Let It Roll*, followed by *Representing the Mambo*. Little Feat has been road and recording dogs ever since, serving up boogie-fried blues and deranged New Orleans grooves as only they can. And Hayward has continued to refine his drumming style with Little Feat and as a hired gun on recordings by Buddy Guy, Eric Clapton, David Garfield, Tinsley Ellis, and Walter Trout.

GEAR & SETUP

Hayward purchased his first set from Montgomery Ward department store with $150 he made from mowing lawns and shoveling rocks. In the late '80s he played a big Pearl Masters Custom kit: two snare drums—a 3.5×14 free-floating piccolo and a 6.5×14 Mahogany Classic Limited Edition, 10×10, 10×12, and 11×13 mounted toms, 12×14 and 14×16 floor toms, and an 18×22

CHECKLIST ✓

❏ **Drums**
Pearl Masters Series, DW, Sabian cymbals

❏ **Condition**
New

❏ **Sticks**
Pro Mark 747

❏ **Setup**
Sits very low, cymbals set high over kit

❏ **Effects**
Zilch

❏ **Feel**
Deep bottomed beat, New Orleans infused

❏ **Signature traits**
Makes odd meters flow as easily as 4/4, inventive use of toms and bass drum within the groove, masterful second-line snare drum work, massive drum sound, deep groove, supple cymbal work

❏ **Influences**
Sonny Payne, Jack Sterling, Max Roach, Art Blakey, Zigaboo Modeliste

❏ **Overall approach**
Brings a New Orleans approach to seminal rock 'n' roll; easily adapts to odd meters, R&B and fusion feels with an undeniably unique sound and style; quirky, funky, futuristic

bass drum. Heads were Remo-coated Ambassador on snare batter with an Ambassador on the snares side, clear Ambassadors top and bottom for toms, and Powerstroke 3s on the bass drum. Cymbals were Sabian, his late '80s complement consisting of 14" AA hi-hats, 10" AA Mini Chinese, 10" AA Splash, 20" Chinese, 12" Splash, 18" AA Crash, 16" El Sabor, 21" AA Medium Ride, 18" El Sabor, 14" Fusion hi-hats, and a 20" AA Chinese.

Hayward's current Drum Workshop VLT setup is finished in Exotic Finish Mapa Burl with a Hard Satin Rich Red Fade and Satin Chrome hardware. Dimensions are 5.5×14 snare, 7×8, 8×10, and 9×12 mounted toms, 12×14 and 14×16 floor toms, an 18×22 bass drum with double tom mount and an 8×22 subwoofer. His DW hardware includes (5) 9700 cymbal boom stands, a 9999 single tom and cymbal stand, 9300 snare stand, 9002 double pedal, 9500 hi-hat, 778 dogbones (1 for cymbal, 4 for mics), and a 934S short boom cymbal arm. Hayward's current Sabian cymbal compliment is a 10" AA Splash, 14" AA X-Celarator, 17" HH Crash, 18" HH Crash, 19" HHX Crash, 18" HHX China, 20" HHX China, and a 20" El Sabor Ride.

Hayward's drums are always tuned very deeply and his snare is especially crisp. This gives his already punchy sound even more extension and dynamics. Ace producers like Ted Templeman brought out Hayward's rich, low-end sound.

STYLE & TECHNIQUE

Maturing as a drummer as Little Feat progressed stylistically, Hayward incorporated the jazz leanings and '50s rock 'n' roll of his youth, the New Orleans influence of his early Little Feat years, and the odd meters and progressive funk of the fusion period. Whew! Only an alignment of the stars and serious talent could have produced the weirdly wonderful grooves Hayward created, but without the free-thinking members of Little Feat—who pushed him to try different ways of playing standard beats—it might have never happened. Part of his approach came as a way to fool Lowell George into thinking

Hayward was playing it straight, when he was really creating new ways of performing fills.

"I always tried to sneak my fills in," Hayward told *Modern Drummer* in 1988. "One of the things I do a lot is to play fills between my left hand and right foot, instead of breaking up the whole feel and doing a fill like it is separate from the groove. That began happening mainly because Lowell kept telling me not to play fills, because he wanted to keep the feel. The only way I could sneak in the fills that I felt were necessary to progress the tune was by doing things with my left hand and right foot. That way the groove didn't get completely broken. It turned into something cool, so I worked it out from there.

"I always thought the bass drum wasn't just the timekeeper," he continued. "It's another part of the instrument. I use the bass drum like a tom; it expands the textures of the kit. I practice various forms of paradiddles between my left hand and right foot and other combinations of ones, twos and threes between the left hand and right foot. [It's] interesting to do little flurries around the bass line—within the groove—where you are not breaking the ride with your right hand, but doing little fills with your left hand and right foot on different drums."

A good example of Little Feat's voluptuous weirdness and Hayward's command of odd meters and unusual ideas is "The Fan," by the drummer's admission the most difficult track he ever played with Little Feat. Flowing through diverse odd meters over a pulsating organ riff and an elastic groove, "The Fan" is like some lost cosmic Allman Brothers Band tune, its bubbling synth and organ notes accompanied by a Zappa-ish guitar solo. Hayward sails through the track with equal parts grace and fire, navigating the odd meters with ease and adding declarative eighth-note triplets (and some flapping tom fills) that help to propel and break up the various sections. His percolating ride cymbal guides the rhythm, while his stabbing snare, toms, and bass drum fills hold down the fort, and then some. Throughout, the odd meters never feel odd, but flow as easily as 4/4.

"There are only two bars of four in the whole song and it switches time signatures," Hayward told *Modern Drummer*. "One of the challenges was playing the fast 7/8 feel and improvising on it under the solo. There's one phrase in ten and a couple in what sounds like eight, but it's really sixteen chopped up into different segments."

Other tracks that reveal Hayward's in total command of unusual time signatures include "Mercenary Territory" (10/4), "Cold Cold Cold" (deftly placed bars of 2/4), and "Day at the Dog Races" (6/4). Never before, or perhaps since, has a rock band played odd meters with such a soulful strut, a wink, and a nod. But even (or perhaps especially) when playing straight time, Hayward adds beautifully deft touches that make his rhythms stand out, like his eighth-note role reversal of snare and hi-hat in "Old Folk's Boogie," the cymbal grabs and hi-hat pushes of "Keepin' Up with the Joneses," the off-beat accents and syncopated backbeat of "Easy to Slip," his absolutely tremendous, end-of-the-world entrance in "Cold Cold Cold," the bump-a-licious second line of "Fat Man in the Bathtub," the story telling groove of "Truck Stop Girl," on and on and on.

LESSON

To capture the style of Richie Hayward is no easy task. Absorb the second-line skills of the Dirty Dozen Brass Band and Paul Barbarian, the suppleness of jazz's bop period, the dry fatback drumming of Sam Lay (Howlin' Wolf), the fusion of Omar Hakim and Alex Acuna (Weather Report), perhaps the slippery hi-hat of Stewart Copeland with the massive pocket of John Bonham. And don't forget your odd meters.

Essentials

▶ Seminal rock 'n' roll beats of Sandy Nelson, Hal Blaine, and Jim Gordon
▶ Playing grooves slightly behind the beat but with scorching propulsion
▶ Odd meter studies
▶ Become fluid displacing eighth-notes as fills and within the groove
▶ Second line snare drum patterns
▶ Understand the jazz fluidity of Art Blakey, Max Roach, and Philly Joe Jones

Example 1

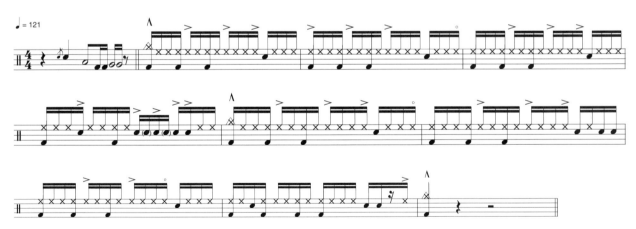

This mighty groove says it all: a New Orleans second-line bass drum rhythm, a fat snare drum thud on *four* of the bar, and tom fills as smooth and seamless as an ocean wave. Donnie's declarative opening fill (a quarter-note accent on *two* and *three*, 16th-note bass drum kicks and two hearty 16th-note floor tom smacks) leads to 16th-note hi-hat variations and one steamrolling beat. Snare stabs and variations (doubling the brass notes) add color, but make sure the beat really cruises, first and foremost.

Example 2

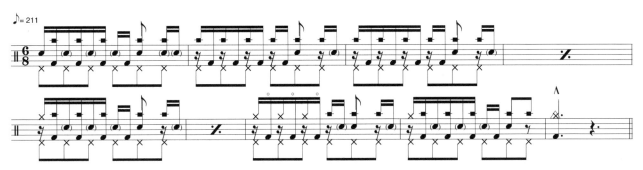

After smacking the snare on the first note of the beat, this tricky 6/8 pattern alternates cymbal bell and bass drum accents within the groove, placing them in unison, then against each other, though the basic 16th-note rhythm never varies. Think of it as a call and response between cymbal bell and bass drum, with the main non-ghosted snare accent (which comes directly after an uplifting 16th-note bass drum) landing literally on the fifth quarter-note of the group of six, matching the keyboard/bass line.

Example 3

Played slightly behind the beat, this gargantuan eighth-note groove erupts with a massively crashing tom fill before settling into an eerily slow-moving pace. Like a lava flow, the beat has both purpose and solidity, and the loping "3 an" snare thwack adds to the suspense. Driving as hard as a tank, this groove is all about feeling the power in the pulse.

Example 4

Hyper New Orleans majesty, coupled with some crazy rock 'n' roll fever. Basically a heavily ghosted 16th-note march pattern (with a shuffle feel) accented on *two* and "uh *four*," it is driven by a 4/4 bass drum pulse and agile knocking of sticks on the snare's metal rims. Play loosely, keeping the sticks very close to head to enable contact with the rims, with higher sticking on the major accents.

CHAPTER 5
Levon Helm

Like an old pair of jeans, a worn tee shirt, and a swinging hammock in summertime, the drumming of Levon Helm just feels good. Levon's combination of heartfelt singing, unique cadence, and Civil War–era drum set (really!) is a virtual rock 'n' roll scrapbook. From his early days with '50s rocker Ronnie Hawkins to his legendary recordings with The Band to his ongoing *Midnight Ramble Sessions*, Levon Helm's drumming is drawn from the very heart of rock 'n' roll, a rustic beat stamped with an Americana trademark.

BIOGRAPHY

Born Mark Lavon Helm on May 26, 1940, in Elaine, Arkansas, "Levon" grew up on a cotton farm listening to radio shows like *The Grand Ole Opry* and *Sonny Boy Williamson and His King Biscuit Entertainers* on Nashville station WLAC. Levon started playing guitar when he was nine, and soon he and his sister

Linda, who played string bass, were entertaining the family and the local 4-H Club with popular songs. When he was 15 Levon saw Elvis Presley perform, and was mightily impressed with his drummer, D.J. Fontana. Soon Levon formed his own band in high school, The Jungle Bush Beaters.

It wasn't until he saw Jerry Lee Lewis' drummer Jimmy Van Eaton (on "Whole Lotta Shakin'") that Levon was convinced to make his own run at the tubs, and listened in earnest to James "Peck" Curtis of Sonny Boy Williamson's band, Elvis' D.J. Fontana, and the New Orleans recordings of Earl Palmer. Lickety-split, he landed a gig with Conway Twitty and his Rock Housers. This led to his first professional gig with Canadian rock 'n' roller Ronnie Hawkins, who was already touring the land in a smart Cadillac. Hawkins signed a record deal in 1959, and he and the band had two big hits, "Forty Days" and "Mary Lou." Slowly the band evolved, and with Levon as a virtual talent scout, they recruited pianist Richard Manuel, bassist Rick Danko, guitarist Robbie Robertson, and organist Garth Hudson, and the nucleus for the act that would become known as The Band had arrived.

Eventually leaving Ronnie in the dust, Levon and the Hawks, as they now called themselves, turned into a crack band with a wealth of musical history, knowledge, and songwriting potential that spread their fame on the Canadian circuit and beyond. Bob Dylan, then considering a change of style from acoustic to electric, drafted The Hawks as his accomplices in this venture. Unfortunately, with folk fans shouting "Judas!" at the unflappable Dylan, Helm didn't enjoy the hostile vibes and returned to Arkansas. When The Hawks, with Dylan in tow, moved to Woodstock, New York, they called Levon and The Band, as they became known around town, and began recording in a small pink house. The Band began working feverishly on material, and with their distance from the centers of musical commerce, both literal and figurative, created a sound based on musical truth, soul, folklore, and rock 'n' roll. Released in 1968, *Music from Big Pink* scored major hits for The Band and had musicians like Eric Clapton and George Harrison singing their praises. The Band's music launched a back-to-the-roots movement among the world's superstar musical elite, who marveled at their depth of soul and pure musicianship. At the core of their sound were the vocals and drumming of Levon Helm, who sang on such hits as "The Weight," and on albums to come, "Cripple Creek," "Rag Mama Rag," and "The Night They Drove Old Dixie Down."

The Band went on to record ten albums with their original lineup, and gave their farewell concert at Winterland in San Francisco on Thanksgiving Day 1976.

Levon cut his first solo album, *Levon Helm & The RCO All-Stars*, in 1977, informed by the same good grooves and folksy tales that had marked his tenure with The Band. And his drumming never sounded better. With his relaxed stage presence, Levon was also a natural in front of the camera, landing roles in the Academy Award–winning films *Coal Miner's Daughter* and *The Right Stuff*. More solo albums followed, including *American Son*, two self-titled albums, and *Souvenir, Vol. 1*. If there was any doubt that Levon played a major role in the success of The Band, his solo albums secured his place as an exceptional drummer, storyteller, singer, multi-instrumentalist, and all-round character.

The Band re-formed, sans Robbie Robertson, in 1983, and after the suicide of Richard Manuel, the remaining trio released 1993's *Jericho*. That same year Helm published his autobiography, *This Wheel's on Fire*, which detailed, among other things, his disgust with Robertson over his wholesale hijacking of The Band's royalties. The albums *High on the Hog* and *Jubilation* followed from The Band. Levon was diagnosed with throat cancer in 1996, but he continued to play drums, mandolin, violin, and harmonica—his music would not be silenced.

By the mid 2000s, Helm had taken up in Woodstock for good and invited his many friends up to play, sing, and generally have a good time. Calling the sessions (and subsequent albums) *The Midnight Ramble Sessions*, Levon surrounded himself with such empathetic entertainers as Emmylou Harris, Elvis Costello, Dr. John, Allan Toussaint, and many more in a repertoire of classic oldtime rockers, country, and R&B favorites and Levon originals.

CHECKLIST ✓

❏ Drums
Yamaha Absolute Birch Nouveau; Zildjian cymbals

❏ Condition
New

❏ Sticks
Pro-Mark 7A

❏ Setup
Sits even with snare, chokes high up on sticks

❏ Effects
Zilch

❏ Feel
Gritty, funky, smacking it in-the-pocket

❏ Signature traits
Ruffs and rolls played with gritty grace; behind-the-beat gumption, digs into the groove *hard*

❏ Influences
D.J. Fontana, Earl Palmer, Jimmy Van Eaton, James "Peck" Curtis

❏ Overall approach
A true original who carved a unique style out of backwoods country, New Orleans rock 'n' roll, and Memphis funk; Levon Helm exemplifies simplicity and soul

SELECTED DISCOGRAPHY

With The Band:

Music from Big Pink
The Band
Stage Fright
Cahoots
Rock of Ages
Moondog Matinee
Northern Lights Southern Cross
Islands
The Last Waltz
Jubilation

Solo albums:

Levon Helm & the RCO All-Stars
The Midnight Ramble Music Sessions, Vols. 1 & 2

RECOMMENDED CUTS

"Up On Cripple Creek" (*The Band*)
"Ophelia" (*Northern Lights—Southern Cross*)
"The Weight" (*Music from Big Pink*)
"The Night They Drove Old Dixie Down" (*The Band*)
"Rag Mama Rag" (*The Band*)
"King Harvest" (*The Band*)
"Chest Fever" (*Music from Big Pink*)
"The Shape I'm In" (*Stage Fright*)
"Life Is a Carnival" (*Cahoots*)
"Ain't Got No Home" (*Moondog Matinee*)

His feverish pocket and good vibes have made Levon an in-demand session drummer, his mighty groove gracing records by Bob Dylan, Ringo Starr, Muddy Waters, Keith Emerson, Joe Walsh, Roger Waters, and Norah Jones.

Odd Fact #1: Elton John's 1971 hit "Levon" was named for the venerable drummer and all-around good guy.

GEAR & SETUP

Levon has played Civil War–era drums tied together with cat gut and wire, classic Slingerland snare drums from the '50s, and old Gretsch and Ludwig kits. But most recently he calls himself a Yamaha man, playing a set of Yamaha Absolute Birch Nouveau on *The Midnight Ramble Sessions*. Dimensions are a 5.5×14 snare, 9×12 mounted tom, 14×14 floor tom, and a 16×20 bass drum. Though he endorses Yamaha hardware, he can also be seen using an old Ludwig Speed King bass drum pedal and occasionally a Sonor snare drum. Zildjian provides his main cymbal complement. Levon uses light, 7A model sticks and Remo drum heads.

Levon sits even with his snare drum. His cymbals are set low, and the drums right below their line of sight. He plays both match and traditional grip, and chokes up rather high on his sticks. He uses as little energy as possible, but gets maximum sound and tone out of his drums.

Levon told *Modern Drummer* magazine in the early 1980s that he liked that "sort of dull 'thud' sound with lots of wood, using the snare for the beat. I like the bass drum kind of toned down, and I usually muffle the toms down a quite a bit more than is usual. On the *Big Pink* album, those tom-tom sounds are tuned a certain way so that they'll dip. You can hit it and the attack dips down; it makes a note and descends.

"You can also do it on a regular drum with plastic heads by loosening the top head and tightening the bottom head. The bottom head needs to be as tight as the top head is loose. Then you get right opposite each other on two of your lugs and you start with your fingers, not a key, to tighten down. Then you can see it, especially under a florescent light and in a studio where the vibrations will form. The skin will be too loose everywhere except for a thin band right across the middle of the drum. You tighten the little band, you hit it, you'll see the vibrations run across the drum and it will hit that band of tenseness. There's where it will catch, make the sound, and then leave that and dip down. So you can sit around and play with that; it takes 20 minutes of fooling with it.

"I will usually throw a wallet on the snare drum, or a cloth, a towel, or tape."

STYLE & TECHNIQUE

Like Charlie Watts and Ringo Starr, Levon Helm is a self-taught drummer who naturally filled the role of perfect timekeeper and creative muse for the musicians that surrounded him.

But there is no nice way to say it: Levon Helm doesn't look natural behind a set of drums. He hunches his shoulders and cracks the snare drum at odd angles. His body lurches in peculiar positions and his arms in particular are good examples of slack motion. Like a preying mantis huddled over a meal, Levon looks too weak and frail to make much of an impact, but as is sometimes the case, looks are deceiving. His groove is as wide as the Mississippi and just as deep. Perhaps in Levon's weird embrace of the drums we are seeing a hundred years of musical history, of Civil War drummers pounding a lone snare drum tattoo, Dixieland drummers wailing a bass battery, or a Deep South rhythm and blues man smacking his skins with nothing but groove in his gut. Levon Helm exemplifies all these styles and genres, going deeper than most drummers, yet without much technique or grasp or rudimental fundamentals to speak of. He's all musical grace and gumption, soul and fire, folklore and rhythmic endurance.

"For me," he told *Modern Drummer*, "that late, leave a pocket for the backbeat style is the Memphis way of playing, like they do in Muscle Shoals. It's a country, R&B feel. Maybe it's the old echo that was on the Sun Records or something—that old doghouse bass fiddle before a snare drum, when it would slap on those records. It does sound most comfortable and it feels the best to me when I can get it right in there and just when it hits in that real soft spot. That gives it breathing room and it keeps the dynamics of the song in proportion."

Levon often plays ruffs, drags, and rolls that are reminiscent of a Civil War drummer. Not marching band cadences with their high, exact stickings, but low-to-the-head, gravelly rudimental notions straight from Appomattox. Like a medium channeling the ghost of a funeral procession, Levon lays it down and burns it clean. He feels everything in his skinny frame and pushes it out, full of life and emphatic.

LESSON

To play like Levon Helm one must relax and *become* the groove. Feel the beat, forget the chops and just put it to the floor. Listen to Levon on classic Band tracks and delve deep into his country state of mind. Imagine you never heard a rudiment, but that the snare drum is your main vehicle of expression, your voice to the world. Levon often plays an entire kit's worth of rhythm on the snare drum, both hands riding and accenting, his body swaying in deep concentration. Simplicity, musicality, and southern fried soul are on the menu.

Essentials

▶ Studying the seminal rock 'n' roll of Little Richard, Jerry Lee Lewis, and the blues of Sonny Boy Williamson and Muddy Waters

▶ Press rolls, drag, ruffs, and ratamacues

▶ Focus on two and four

▶ Swing triplets between snare and toms

Example 1

Track 18

Big tom accents played with a very deliberate delivery on *three* and *four* lead into this grandly powerful beat. Simple to be sure, but played with a soulful sense of purpose, and perhaps lightly behind the beat. It ain't called "The Weight" for nothing.

Example 2

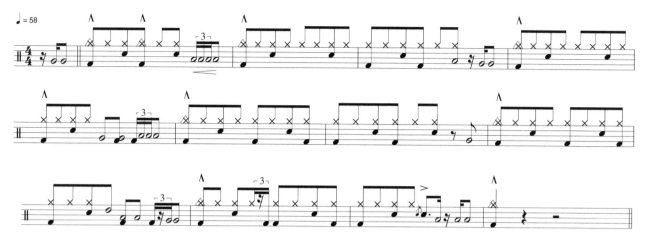

Performed similarly to Ex. 1, but even slower, and with the eighth-note riding pattern played on the cymbal. Small tom fills give the beat space and detail, allowing the drummer to really feel the groove and add color where needed. Slow down and feel the pulse.

Example 3

This super-funky quasi second line beat actually begins by replicating a two-handed snare march on the full kit, then drops the literal beat altogether but not the pulse, maintaining this good-feeling groove with sprightly fills that are trickier to execute than they sound. Here, Levon Helm's bouncing tom fills recall the sparking tom work of Derek and the Dominoes' Jim Gordon, a master at making a groove truly *move*. The main groove returns, but it's the tom fills that push it along.

Example 4

Another tricky groove, in the nature of its squirming, jumping-ahead-of-the-beat tom fills. It sounds simple enough in its 4/4 punch, but every other snare beat is dropped, while the bass drum is the main rhythmic mover. It's the 16th double on *two* that makes the groove stand out. A little beat turn-around later in the bars ramps up the level of difficulty, but focus on making the groove jump.

CHAPTER 6
Mitch Mitchell

 An explosive drummer who created a new style of rock drumming in the '60s influenced as much by jazz legend Elvin Jones as his own time and beat conceptions, Mitch Mitchell became a star with Jimi Hendrix, then virtually disappeared. Brandishing a liquid, jazz-inspired pulse in the trademark Hendrix vehicles "Manic Depression," "Foxy Lady," "Third Stone from the Sun," "Up from the Skies," "Fire," and "Crosstown Traffic," Mitch Mitchell plied finesse and ferociousness with a flashy demeanor that perfectly complemented Hendrix's wild stage antics, powerful psychedelia, and innovative musicianship. Perhaps no other rock drummer has matched Mitchell's combination of swinging jazz figures and combustible rock groove, surpassing even Ginger Baker for pure dotted eighth-note bravado and swing triplet prowess. Baker brought 1940s big band drumming to rock; Mitchell integrated the '60s jazz innovations of Elvin Jones, Tony Williams, and Joe Morello, catapulting rock drumming into the cosmos, perhaps further than it has been before or since.

BIOGRAPHY

Born on July 9, 1947, in Ealing, Middlesex (England), John Mitch Mitchell was involved in the arts from a young age. As a teenager he played Macbeth on BBC radio, hosted his own TV series, *Jennings in School*, and portrayed the original Artful Dodger character in the West End production of *Oliver*. Though not formally trained on the drums, Mitchell's career was booming by the age of 13, when he played in such bands as Pete Nelson and the Travellers, Chris Stanford's Riot Squad, Georgie Fame's Blue Flames, and he even recorded with the Pretty Things.

In the fall of 1966 guitarist Jimi Hendrix arrived in London to audition drummers for his new trio. Fortuitously, Georgie Fame had recently fired his entire band, freeing Mitchell to audition for the Hendrix slot. Only 19 and very confident, Mitchell's biggest competition for the gig was studio drummer Aynsley Dunbar (who would eventually make his name with Frank Zappa and Jefferson Starship). A coin toss decided Mitchell's fate. Mitchell played it safe in the audition, but by the time rehearsals commenced one month later, he began to open up. Mitchell's ability to match Hendrix in levels of musical freedom and improvisation was explosive nearly from the start. Their rapport was instantaneous. The Jimi Hendrix Experience became one of the world's first "power trios." Matching Hendrix for power, speed and soloing capability, Mitchell, like Elvin Jones (with Coltrane) and Max Roach (with Charlie Parker) before him, was the perfect rhythmic foil and creative impetus for the guitarist's amazing melodic inventions.

The Experience continued to rehearse in London (with guitarist turned bassist Noel Redding), performing on their first television show in Paris in October 1966, followed by an appearance on the British pop staple *Ready, Steady, Go!* They debuted their fantastic live show at the Bag O'Nails in early 1967. Soon thereafter they recorded what would become *Are You Experienced?*, a pivotal album in rock 'n' roll history. Merging soulful, spacey rock with elastic jams and searing psychedelia, the Experience were easily the most daring and exciting band of their day, and their soloing was without peer, even amid rock monsters like The Who or Cream, who played more of a blues-based, power-rock style of improvisation. Hendrix and Mitchell played in a lighter, less bombastic style closer to the then nascent free jazz movement, and thus cast their webs much wider. While Cream was more grounded and boisterous, the Jimi Hendrix Experience was free to explore, float, and fly.

The Hendrix trio played the 1967 Monterey Pop Festival, culminating in a fiery performance of The Trogg's "Wild Thing," which ended with Jimi setting his guitar on fire with lighter fluid. Shortly thereafter, the Experience signed to open a U.S. tour for teen pop idols The Monkees—Hendrix and Co. departed within weeks. The Experience began sessions for their second album, *Axis: Bold as Love*, in America, then returned to London to continue recording. The album was released in December 1967, cementing the group's international success.

The Experience was now touring incessantly when not recording; the sessions for the double LP *Electric Ladyland* beginning in January 1968. As Hendrix's songs grew ever more extravagant and visionary, bassist Noel Redding became more restless, departing mid-session. Redding was replaced by various players, but Mitchell remained a constant, and grew in stature and ambition, just as Hendrix progressed musically. Many tracks were cut by Mitchell and Hendrix performing alone in the studio, with other musicians overdubbing parts. *Electric Ladyland* showed Hendrix moving away from a simple pop framework into the realm of full-blown studio epics, reflecting the era's penchant for experimentation. But Hendrix, with Mitchell by his side, took it further out than anyone thought possible with stunning tracks like "1983: A Mermaid I Should Turn to Be" and "Voodoo Child (Slight Return)."

After *Electric Ladyland* was released, Mitchell capitalized on his fame by performing as a member of the Dirty Mac on the (then unreleased) *Rolling Stones Rock and Roll Circus*. Comprised of John Lennon, Keith Richards, Eric Clapton, and Mitchell, the Dirty Mac played a blistering version of The Beatles'

CHECKLIST ✓

❏ **Drums**
Premier, Ludwig, Gretsch; Zildjian cymbals

❏ **Condition**
New

❏ **Sticks**
Ludwig 5A

❏ **Setup**
Sits even with snare, hunched over kit

❏ **Effects**
Zilch

❏ **Feel**
Airy and propulsive

❏ **Signature traits**
Blazingly fast single- and double-stroke rolls, great freedom around the kit, engrossing improvisations, inventive tom and full set patterns mirroring Hendrix's innovative approach

❏ **Influences**
Elvin Jones, Tony Williams

❏ **Overall approach**
A major drum innovator whose jazz-inspired approach widened the possibilities of rock drumming and seeded the fusion movement that followed

SELECTED DISCOGRAPHY

With the Jimi Hendrix Experience:

Are You Experienced?
Axis: Bold As Love
Electric Ladyland
First Rays of the New Rising Sun
BBC Sessions

RECOMMENDED CUTS

"Foxy Lady" (*Are You Experienced?*)
"Manic Depression" (*Are You Experienced?*)
"Purple Haze" (*Are You Experienced?*)
"Crosstown Traffic" (*Greatest Hits*)
"Third Stone from the Sun" (*Greatest Hits*)
"Spanish Castle Magic" (*Axis: Bold as Love*)
"Up from the Skies" (*Axis: Bold as Love*)
"Little Wing" (*Axis: Bold as Love*)
"Hey Joe" (*Are You Experienced?*)

"Yer Blues," the drummer driving the Lennon/Clapton solo section with a manically pointed 6/8 ride cymbal pattern that nearly pushed the band off the stage.

The Experience, with Redding back in the fold for PR concerns, reformed to play a London TV show in early 1969, and then began sessions for their ultimately unreleased fourth album at Olympic Studios. They played two shows at Royal Albert Hall, Hendrix's final London shows until the band's Isle of Wight performance in September 1970. Redding left for good soon enough, replaced by Hendrix's old army buddy Billy Cox. The band then performed under a new name, Gypsy Sun and Rainbows. They played their famous Woodstock show in August, augmented by a full percussion section and a second guitarist. Though the performance was a massive success, the band took the stage so late in the evening that Mitchell's hands were ice cold.

Returning to London, Mitchell took on session work (Fat Mattress, Eire Apparent, Martha Velez) and also played with Jack Bruce and Friends. Mitchell was also invited to a very loose jam session at Miles Davis' house, where guitarist John McLaughlin was in attendance. Mitchell rejoined Hendrix after Band of Gypsys (with Buddy Miles and Billy Cox) disbanded, and the trio of Hendrix, Mitchell, and Cox played California in early 1970 using the original name, The Jimi Hendrix Experience, and alternately, Cry of Love. They returned to Hendrix's Electric Lady studios in New York to continue work on the fourth album, recording a mind-blowing amalgam of jazz, rock, blues, and funk. During this time keyboardist Keith Emerson asked Mitchell to join the band that would eventually become Emerson, Lake and Palmer. He also asked Hendrix to join the lineup, but he and Mitchell declined. The Experience continued to tour right up to Hendrix's death on September 18, 1970.

The Experience was in the middle of a break when Mitchell and Ginger Baker, joined by Sly (of Sly and the Family Stone), were to meet up with

Hendrix for a loose jam session (with recording possibilities in mind) at a London bar known as the Speakeasy. Hendrix failed to show, and the following afternoon Mitchell received a phone call confirming the death of the master guitarist; he died in his sleep after a drug overdose.

Later Mitchell attended sessions to clean up and overdub his drumming to Hendrix songs that were still in production, including "Angel," "Drifting," and "Belly Button Window." In 1972 Mitchell redid the part for "Stepping Stone." These tunes and others appeared on 1997's *First Rays of the New Rising Sun,* which sought to recreate Hendrix's original intent for his incomplete fourth album.

After Hendrix's death, Mitchell joined Ramatam (a band meant to capitalize on the fame of Mitchell and Blues Image guitarist Mike Pinera) and worked the occasional studio session, but for all intents and purposes, he dropped off the map. This was certainly one of the oddest career moves ever, as Mitchell obviously had the technique and talent to play with anyone, and his profile was never higher. He later recorded with Jack Bruce, Muddy Waters, Roger Chapman, Randy California, Carl Perkins, and David Torn. In 1990 he wrote *Jimi Hendrix: Inside the Experience*, detailing his time with the Experience; most recently he performed with the Gypsy Sun Experience band with Billy Cox.

Mitch Mitchell is currently retired and lives in Europe.

GEAR & SETUP

Throughout his career Mitch Mitchell played several different brands of kit, including Premier, Ludwig, and Gretsch. His main kit was a Premier set, including 14×22 bass drum, 5.5×14 Premier 2000 metal snare, 8×14 mounted tom, and 14×14 and 16×16 floor toms. His Zildjian cymbal compliment was simpler than most: 14" hi-hats, 16" crash, 18" crash ride, and 20" ride with rivets (he later switched to larger 22" or 24" rides). His silver sparkle Ludwig set was nearly identical in dimensions, but with a 20" bass drum and 9×13 mounted tom. He adopted a Ludwig double-bass-drum kit with 24" kicks, but stuck with a single 8×12 mounted tom. And as can be seen on the *Rock and Roll Circus* DVD, Mitchell also played a Gretsch kit of similar dimensions. Displaying some of the worst posture ever, Mitchell typically sat even with the snare drum but very hunched over the kit.

STYLE & TECHNIQUE

Even with his lack of rudimental training, Mitch Mitchell displayed excellent control and technique, even if was not a powerful drummer by today's standards. He was very flexible and used both traditional and matched grip as needed, executing very fast and exciting fills with either grip. His live performances with Hendrix show a drummer able to spin time on a dime, mirroring the guitarist note-for-note in burning double and single-stroke rolls, bass drum/tom-tom full set triplets, and solid jazz interpretation ("Third Stone from the Sun"). Mitchell also plays wonderfully erudite brushes on "Up from the Skies," swinging around the kit, accenting with hi-hat accents, and even double-timing the fills around the kit at one point.

Mitchell's time feel could be very punchy, placing bass drum accents with the agility of a jazz player, and not a little influenced by Ginger Baker. Mitchell also played with incredible finesse, often playing snare and tom combinations with a light, almost wispy touch that belied his powerful role with the Experience. By contrast he could drive a song extremely hard, as heard on "Voodoo Child (Slight Return)" and the live version of "Fire" from *The Jimi Hendrix Experience BBC Sessions*. Here, Mitchell slashes the hi-hat while playing loping funk patterns interspersed with his trademark swinging tom fills and fiery cymbal crashes. On the same recording he is considerably funky on "Little Miss Lover," cuts loose with some serious Latin figures on "Love or Confusion," and steamrolls his kit to madness on "Killing Floor."

Along with "Little Wing" and "Crosstown Traffic," perhaps the song most associated with Mitch Mitchell is "Manic Depression." Beginning with snare and tom rolls that alternately descend and ascend around the kit to accompany the opening guitar riff, Mitchell then breaks up the main 6/8 groove by playing an eighth-note cymbal bell pattern with ghost-notes on the snare and toms with the bass drum on the downbeat. Mitchell practically flies around the kit; executing storming 16th-note triplet fills (often breaking up the time) in the rests, climaxing in a full set barrage during Hendrix's solo. Smashing cymbals and accelerating the tom figures (doubling the 6/8 pulse briefly in live versions) while maintaining the song's blistering pulse, Mitchell creates one of rock's most enduring and exciting drum patterns.

LESSON

To play like Mitch Mitchell one must divide his studies equally between jazz and rock. Absorbing the above-the-kit feel of Elvin Jones and Tony Williams and seamlessly integrating with the earthen rock truncheons of John Bonham (and Ginger Baker) and the funk of Bernard Purdie, the Mitchell style is adaptable, kinetic, explosive.

Essentials

- ▶ Jazz studies of Elvin Jones, Tony Williams, Joe Morello
- ▶ Single- and double-stroke rolls, flams, and rudimental studies
- ▶ Rudimental workouts for speed and control
- ▶ Swing triplets between snare and toms
- ▶ Full-set triplets between bass drums and toms
- ▶ Fluid funk patterns à la Bernard Purdie, rock re John Bonham and Ginger Baker

Example 1

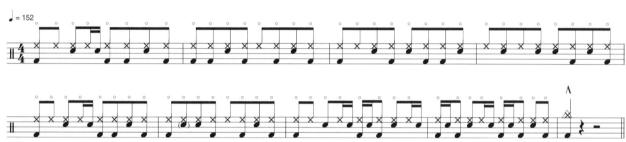

Loose hi-hats bashed in an eighth-note stream and a funky bass drum popping down below, this famous beat is really just Clyde Stubblefield (of James Brown's Fabulous Flames) ramped up for freaky '60s psychedelia. The tightly tuned snare is played mostly as rim shots, and Stubblefield's "Funky Drummer" routine is referenced throughout (think a funky boogaloo if you go back that far). Thirty years later that beat would be sped up for drum and bass boffins the world over.

Example 2

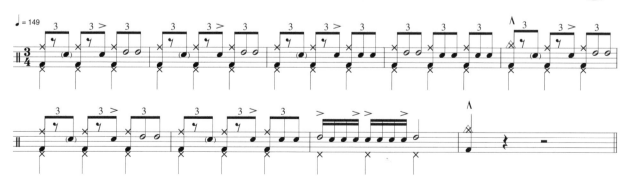

A 3/4 groove played with manic intensity, this one is simpler than it sounds, at least as far as the basic notation is concerned. The bass drum and bell are played in unison on the quarter-notes, with the left hand playing the second two grace notes of the triplet on the snare. The tough part is slapping the hard snare accent on the "uh" after *two* and the "an uh" after *three*, into the soon arriving downbeat of the next bar. This one is all about flow, so practice playing the left-hand figures on the snare drum at first, paying attention to the two different stick heights to separate the grace notes from the main accents.

Example 3

Track
24

This flailing, fighting beat is the template for the metal machinations that would come some 30 years later. Mitchell's eighth-note smashing, trashing, and pummeling of the crashes as the main locomotive of the beat add color and life to the straight rock groove that steamrolls underneath.

Example 4

Track
25

A long, beautiful row of 16th-note triplets opens this powerful groove, and they have been imitated by every drummer who has ever played this classic song. Practice playing the bass drum on *one* and *three* as you break up the triplets: *one* on the tom and the other two ghost-notes on the snare. The tricky part is to feel the flow: the triplets don't begin on the downbeat, but on the last note of the triplet before the downbeat. Once mastered, this slightly displaced sticking can make many beats flow and gives you a cool tool to twist around songs. Hendrix gave Mitchell a lot of room to roam on "Little Wing"; he created high drumming art.

CHAPTER 7
Keith Moon

Often described as rock's supreme madman cum flamboyant clown, and alternately as a "dear boy" who was somehow not in proper control of his own facilities—mental, physical, or otherwise—Keith Moon was one of rock's greatest and most influential drummers—he also represents one of its undisputed tragedies. Moon's galvanic drumming was like the sound of a hundred Zeppelins crashing down a mountainside or the glee of a child bashing a monstrous kit in 4/4 time. He was a force of nature who lived to pound his bass drum like a tank while flailing at the rest of his kit like it owed him money. Moon's drumming created a vocabulary for every rock drummer that followed, his hurricane of fills, smashes, tumbling rolls, and cymbal crashes laying bedrock for the punk, surf, and free-form garage rock to come. Though rock drummers for generations would claim him as an influence, Moon's favorite drummers were big-band icons, Gene Krupa and Buddy Rich.

"When you see Moon playing mad breaks," said Who bassist John Entwistle, according to www.keithmoon.co.uk, "he's not going around the kit, his arms are moving forward from the snare to the toms; I've never seen anyone play like that before or since."

Moon was the cornerstone of The Who's nascent punk sound, matching guitarist Pete Townsend's aggression and volume while driving every song with the same zeal that possessed Entwistle. He was the legendarily frenetic pulse and irrepressible power behind such classic Who hits as "Tommy," "Won't Get Fooled Again," "Love, Reign O'er Me," "Pinball Wizard," "My Generation," and "I Can See for Miles."

BIOGRAPHY

Keith Moon was born Keith John Moon on August 23, 1946, to Alfred and Kathleen Moon in Wellesden, England. As a child young Keith was as enamored of Nat King Cole as of the BBC comedy troupe the Goons, even then expressing a desire to match music with mayhem. Moon played trumpet in a drum and bugle corps, at 13 switching to the bass drum. He received his first full-sized kit, a pearl blue Premier setup, in 1961 and by the following year was already in his first band, the Escorts, followed shortly by the Beachcombers. Two years later and already a veteran of the local band circuit, Moon was asked to join The Who, a band who at the time didn't seem to have much of a future against the then popular surf rock scene (popularized by the Shadows).

During a residency at the Railway club in 1964, Moon began kicking, bashing, overturning, and generally destroying his drums in response to similar antics from guitarist Pete Townsend. Moon later stated, "When I've smashed my drums it's because I was pissed off…when you've worked your balls off and given the audience everything and they don't give anything back, that's when the [expletive deleted] instruments go." It was all part of The Who's youthful credo of "Auto Destruction." Years later, during an appearance on the *Smothers Brothers* television show, Moon loaded his bass drum with explosives, which were detonated during the end of "My Generation," causing permanent hearing damage to Townsend.

The Who released their debut *My Generation* album in 1965, followed by the early '66 single "Substitute." Already reveling in the excess, Moon moved from a smallish single-bass-drum, seven-piece Premier kit to his first double-bass-drum, nine-piece setup. The Who's albums flowed fast and furious, with every release Moon becoming more explosive, inspired, and creative than the last. "Happy Jack" hit in 1966; in '67 Moon played on Jeff Beck's single "Beck's Bolero." That same year Moon showcased his custom-built "Pictures of Lily" Premier drum kit with its comic message emblazoned on the bass drum head: "Keith Moon Patent British Exploding Drummer." The Who soon made a major splash at the Monterey Pop Festival, where, of course, Moon laid waste to his kit to close the show in truly bombastic style. *The Who Sell Out* was released in '67 as well, followed two years later by the band's magnum-opus rock opera, *Tommy*, and its major U.S. radio hit "Pinball Wizard." The song's B-side, a Moon composition, featured a dog barking lead vocals.

In 1970, a few months after a triumphant Who performance at the Woodstock festival, and with his alcohol intake at a peak (living up to his nickname, "Moon the Loon"), Moon accidentally drove his Bentley over Cornelius "Neil" Boland, his chauffeur, killing him almost instantly. As Boland had tried to clear the way for Moon to exit a club, he fell beneath the wheels of the drummer's car. Afraid of the growing crowd and unaware of Boland's fall, Moon stepped on the accelerator and rolled over his driver. Moon was charged with vehicular manslaughter, but was later acquitted.

Now a bona fide worldwide success, The Who released *Live at Leeds* in 1970, followed by the classic *Who's Next* in '71 and the ambitious rock opera *Quadrophenia* in '73. During downtime between albums Moon made his acting debut in Frank Zappa's *200 Motels* (appearing as a nun fearful of overdosing on pills) and performed in a series of BBC radio shows called *Life with the Moons*, which included comic routines and selections of Moon's favorite music. In '73 Moon's wife, Kim, left him, further accelerating his slide into alcohol and substance abuse. This added to now infamous stories of Moon's madness, such as dressing up as Adolf Hitler, running naked through airports, destroying hotel rooms, throwing televisions out of hotel windows, fainting at various locations, and as always, imbibing large amounts of alcohol. Moon continued to accept acting roles, including that of Uncle Ernie in the film version of *Tommy* and as Buddy Holly drummer J.D. Clover in *Stardust*. Moon moved to LA in hopes of finding a full-on acting career, and it was here that he also recorded his lone solo effort, *Two Sides of Moon* (1975), an album of rock 'n' roll covers that handed most of the drumming chores to Ringo Starr and Jim Keltner. While in Los Angeles, Moon also hosted a weekend variety show, *In Concert*, playing a drum solo while goldfish swam around his bass drum turned aquarium.

The Who by Numbers, which debuted in 1975, showed the band slowly running out of steam, the pressure of worldwide superstardom and the hedonistic rock 'n' roll lifestyle taking its toll. Or perhaps The Who, now ten years on, had simply run its course. Only one song from the album, "Squeezebox," climbed into the U.S. Top 20. Keith Moon's final album with The Who was 1978's *Who Are You*, its cover featuring Moon sitting in a chair with the words NOT TO BE TAKEN AWAY visible on its back cushion. The album's quality was mixed, but Moon was in fine form on the album's lone hit and title track, "Who Are You."

Moon's end came on the night of September 6, 1978, when he attended a party in London held by Paul and Linda McCartney for the premiere of *The Buddy Holly Story*. Not feeling well, Moon, with his girlfriend, Annette Walter-Lax, returned to his apartment at #9, 12 Curzon Place. It is reported that he had a glass of white wine and watched a bit of *The Abominable Dr. Phibes* before turning in to bed. Moon died in his sleep. He was found the next morning, and it was determined that he had overdosed on the anti-seizure medication Heminevrin, which had been prescribed as part of a program to wean Moon off alcohol. A postmortem confirmed there were 32 tablets in Moon's system, 26 of them undissolved. Keith Moon was 32.

GEAR & SETUP

Keith Moon played many, many, many different sets between 1965 and 1978, though his allegiance to Premier remained largely secure. His early '61 to '65 kits included a four-piece blue pearl Premier "Outfit 55" kit, as well as a silver sparkle Ludwig Super Classic kit, as popularized by Ringo Starr.

Moon played a five-piece Premier kit until early 1967, when he purchased a Premier red pearl double bass kit with three mounted toms and two floor toms, augmented by various Paiste and Zildjian cymbals. The bass drums were locked together by tom mounts, a true relic of '60s drum engineering.

Later in '67, Moon asked Premier to custom-build a double-bass-drum kit that would become known as the "Pictures of Lily" set. Featuring pictures of Moon surrounded by cherubim, the Union Jack, and THE WHO printed

CHECKLIST ✓

❑ Drums
1961: Premier, '64 to '65: Ludwig Super Classic, '65 to '73: expanding Premier kits, '70 to '71: clear Zickos, '73 to '78: Premier

❑ Condition
New

❑ Sticks
Ajax E, Premier C

❑ Setup
Sits high off the set

❑ Effects
Mallets, large gong, tympani, concert toms, triangle, claves

❑ Feel
Explosive, forward-moving, huge groove, bombastic, grandiose

❑ Signature traits:
Driving eighth-note bass drum figures, spastic body contortions, manic single-stroke tom rolls, theatrical showmanship

❑ Influences
Gene Krupa, Buddy Rich

❑ Overall approach
A blinding sense of energy and forward motion resulting in a skirmish of cymbal crashes, thunderous tom fills, and splattering beats

SELECTED DISCOGRAPHY

With The Who:

Tommy
Quadrophenia
Who's Next
Who Are You
My Generation
The Who Sell Out
Magic Bus
Live at Leeds

With Jeff Beck:

Truth

Solo albums:

Two Sides of Moon

RECOMMENDED CUTS

"Pinball Wizard" (*Tommy*)
"Won't Get Fooled Again" (*Who's Next*)
"My Generation" (*My Generation*)
"The Real Me" (*Quadrophenia*)
"Baba O'Riley" (*Who's Next*)
"Bargain" (*Who's Next*)
"My Wife" (*Who's Next*)
"I Can See for Miles" (*The Who Sell Out*)
"Love, Reign O'er Me" (*Quadrophenia*)
"Magic Bus" (*Magic Bus*)
"Summertime Blues" (*Live at Leeds*)

in letters that arose, Superman style, from somewhere beyond the horizon, the psychedelically painted, $5,000 kit was also renowned for the naked photos of a young woman named Lily that adorned its surfaces. Hardware was by Gretsch, with Rogers Swiv-O-Matic tom holders. Premier LokFast stands and a Premier 250 bass drum pedal were augmented by Premier Everplay Extra heads on tom-toms, floor toms, and bass drums. Keith used variations on the dimensions of this kit throughout the early '70s, including a transparent acrylic Zickos drum kit for The Who's 1970 U.S. tour.

From 1973 on, Moon's Premier kits featured two rows of tom-toms: his standard three mounted toms joined by a second tier of six concert toms, plus tympani and gong to the side. By now Moon's cymbals were always Paiste Classic 2002 series with black logo: 15" Heavy hi-hats, 16" crash, 18" crash, 20" crash, 18" medium crash, and 22" ride with various symphonic gongs (30"–38").

Moon's final monster kit heading into the mid to late 1970s was a Premier cream-white-finish design with copper-colored lugs and hardware, dimensions as follows: 5.5×14 metal snare drum, (3) 10×14 mounted toms, (2) 16×16 floor toms, 16×18 floor tom, (2) 14×22 bass drums, concert toms: 8×10, 10×12,12×13,10×14, 14×15, 16×16, (2) timbales, and one 22 ½" tympani. The set was occasionally augmented with an additional pair of mounted floor toms (!) and two Premier 22 ½" tympani. Cymbals were still Paiste 2002, but slightly pared down to smaller dimensions: 22" ride, 20" crash, 14" splash, 18" crash, 14" hi-hat, and one or two Paiste gongs (30", 36").

Moon favored Ludwig Supraphonic 400 snares and often left his hi-hat cymbals half open for proper bashing angle. He used AJAX E and Premier C drumsticks and Premier Everplay Extra drumheads, smooth white finish.

Check out http://www.thewho.net/whotabs/ equipment/drums/equip-moondrums.htm for great pics.

STYLE & TECHNIQUE

As can be seen in various pics of Moon behind the kit, he sat somewhat high off the drums, no doubt the height helping him to flail and contort his body as he slammed the skins from every angle. It has been said that Moon never practiced and that he kept no drum sets at any of his homes. John Entwhistle reportedly said Moon had his own separate rehearsals where he would often take two to three days to re-learn the song's drum parts once they were finalized.

Moon's entire approach, from his grip to his body position, was unorthodox. His unusual, rather delicate grip made it appear as if he was primarily using fingers, as would a timpani player. Photos show Moon (sometimes) pointing his index finger at the top of the stick, with his remaining fingers tightly curled around the shank. He also sometimes played with the back shank of the stick, giving him more power and a blunt tone. His sticks were rather lightweight, which further enabled him to bash and pummel in speedy fashion.

But if his grip seemed slight, his physical impact was not. Moon literally attacked the kit with his whole body. Thrusting himself into the drums, his small frame and small hands were in a whirl of constant motion as he contorted and twisted his body, which both facilitated his uniquely chaotic sound and added a showy flair, which became his trademark.

It is almost impossible to decipher exactly what Moon played on certain tracks. His drumming is like a tornado of 16th-note triplet rhythms played on every source, gracefully flailing over the top of the kit as he pumped a constant stream of eighth-notes on his bass drum, a direct link to his fondness for big-band drummers.

Moon's thrashing fills at the end of "My Generation" are one example of his drumming-blind approach; he seems to be hitting all the toms at once, mixing triplets with pointed accents in a rolling wave of propulsion. "I Can See For Miles" offers a similar journey into full-set mayhem. Bashing the crashes in unison with Pete Townsend's sitar-like guitar accents in the chorus, Moon also plays subtle single-stroke snare drum rolls and resonant tom thuds that add to the rhythmic tension.

"Pinball Wizard" is, of course, one of the greatest tracks in rock, and Moon's performance supplies the song with drama, tension, and grand theatrics. His tom fills leading into the chorus are barely in time, as if Moon got to the toms with a moment to spare. His strikes sound inconsistent, almost weak, but the energy is undeniably Moon. The drums are tuned tightly; Moon begins rolling on the full set before the bridge. "Summertime Blues" is also full-on, Moon crashing cymbals and pounding his toms with manic intensity, unleashing rolling thunder on the toms practically throughout the song. Here, Moon maintains a perpetual-motion machine for the entire song, executing a full assault of volume and drive like an over-caffeinated steamroller.

One of the best recorded examples of Moon's madness is "Won't Get Fooled Again." Here, the drums are mixed front and center, the Premiers sounding especially boingy and sharp. Moon pushes the song along with his usual array of rhythmic one-liners and punch-drunk fills, and his snare work is especially pointed and almost obsessive. He plays fills at every chance, occasionally flaming eighth-note snare patterns in concert with his bass drum. At the 7:30 mark, after an ARP Odyssey plays a series of soothing tones, Moon dropkicks a few ascending tom lines, bringing The Who back into the song; he plays a hard four to the bar pulse out to the final crushing accents and a flurry of cymbal crescendos.

Many have tried to emulate Moon's cacophony, but there is only one Keith Moon.

LESSON

Playing like Keith Moon may be more a state of mind than anything else, with the ability to become very excited, perhaps even traumatized, before you sit down at the kit something to consider. Studying the work of Gene Krupa (the first drum manic) is essential, as is an understanding of his pounding, four-to-the-bar bass drum message. Moon was also a very good timekeeper, though it was the mighty John Entwhistle who maintained the absolute bottom of the band, both sonically and mentally. Full set triplets and crossovers, solid single-stroke roll technique, and a healthy dose of cymbal bashing are other ingredients of the Moon style.

Essentials
► Four-to-the-bar bass drum studies
► Single-stroke rolls incorporating entire kit
► Swing, shuffle, eighth-note rock, and 3/4 waltz patterns
► Full set studies incorporating single-stroke rolls, flams, and ruffs
► Complete rudimental snare studies

Example 1

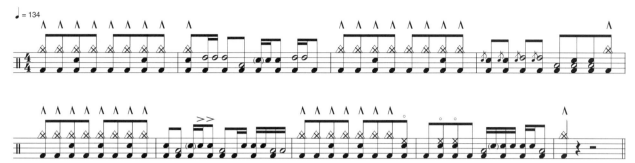

The key to this mad circus of a beat is the driving sequence of eighth-notes on the bass drum and Moon's seeming ability to play every drum and cymbal at once. Actually an old Gene Krupa trick, the chugging bass notes enable the freedom to play all manner of snare and tom swing triplets, around-the-kit flams, and ceaseless cymbal crashes. Of course, this kind of beat is practically a solo in itself, as was the original intention in this manic freak-out anthem.

Example 2

A perfectly standard eighth-note rock groove augmented by a 16th-note hi-hat pattern and a series of flamboyant fill concoctions, as only Moon the Loon could devise.

Example 3

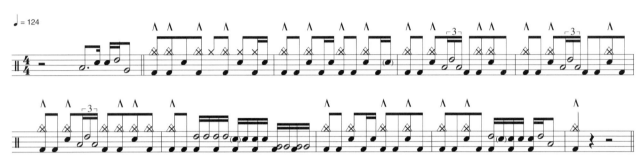

More flailing crash cymbals and the locomotive 1/8th bass drum intent within a quarter-note groove. Fills, fills, fills, but the most deceptive one of all is the 16th-note triplet broken up between all the drums. (R) snare, (L) tom, (R) floor tom, and bass drum played in a flowing manner make this one move like rocket.

Example 4

Keith Moon's stellar ability to roll all over his kit while maintaining a powerful groove remains the biggest mystery of his style. Anyone who attempts it is automatically found out, as Moon's signature sound is recognizable a mile away. This one is similar to "Pinball Wizard"; enjoy the bashing—make sure the groove pops.

CHAPTER 8
Ian Paice

Typically, aspiring drummers spend hours pursuing rudimental studies, perfecting their rolls and paradiddles, creating power reserves and facilitating multi-limbed independence. Other drummers simply relax at the kit, and like magic, do it all as if they were born to play. Ian Paice is a rare example of the latter school, a self-taught drummer whose incredible speed and precision was matched by excellent coordination, creative tom fills, explicitly funky beats, and a big-band-style approach. It is often said that Paice was the first heavy metal drummer, but that is a misnomer. Deep Purple may have been the first heavy metal *band*, but the left-handed Paice was decidedly old school, kicking his English band mates' heavy blues rock with a blowtorch sensibility strictly modeled on the swing triplets and fiery single-stroke rolls of Buddy Rich coupled to the funk of Bernard Purdie. Paice's work on such classic Deep Purple albums as *In Rock*, *Fireball*, *Machine Head*, *Burn*, and *Stormbringer* stands the test of time, revealing the scorch and sweat of a brilliant technician performing at the top of his game

BIOGRAPHY

Ian Anderson Paice has had a long and colorful career, manning the helm of Deep Purple as their only drummer while the band's personnel shifted around him like a game of musical chairs. He was born in Nottingham, England, on June 29, 1948, and began playing drums at the relatively late age of 15, initially joining his father's dance band (his father taught him the basics of a double stroke roll). Paice's early influences included Gene Krupa, Buddy Rich, Ringo Starr, Mitch Mitchell, Carmine Appice, Bobby Elliot (The Hollies), and Ginger Baker.

Paice played with a string of obscure local bands bearing such '60s-style names as Georgie & the Rave Ons, the Shindigs, the MI 5, the Maze, Soul Brothers, and Boz. While playing in one of these nondescript acts (MI 5) in that furnace of '60s rock 'n' roll known as Hamburg, Germany, Paice crossed paths with Blackmore (working with Boz), who would soon audition his band's singer, then ask explicitly for the drummer as well. By 1968 Roundabout had formed, and within a year, having changed their name to Deep Purple, the R&B-infused band had their first global hit single, "Hush."

As the '60s turned to the '70s and the era of grandiose prog- and blues-rock began, Deep Purple was at the forefront of the movement, the band's theatrical organ work, wailing vocals, blistering guitar, and fiery drumming making them one of the most popular bands in the world.

Beginning in 1968, a then 19-year-old Paice played in every incarnation of Deep Purple, originating with that first lineup of guitarist Blackmore, vocalist Rod Evans, organist Jon Lord, and bassist Nick Simper. *Shades of Deep Purple, Book of Taliesyn,* and *Deep Purple* brought this lineup to 1969. The next band, which acquired vocalist Ian Gillian and bassist Roger Glover, lasted until '73. Many consider this to be the classic Deep Purple lineup, which produced *In Rock, Fireball, Machine Head,* and *Who Do We Think We Are.* But for my money, the next version of Deep Purple provided Paice with some of the best source material of his career. The band, which now included vocalist David Coverdale and astutely funky bassist Glenn Hughes, created *Burn* and *Stormbringer* and such amazing Paice-demolishing tracks as "Burn," "Lay Down, Stay Down," "You Fool No One," "Sail Away," "Lady Double Dealer," and "Might Just Take Your Life." Paice is in stellar form throughout, but this incarnation nonetheless gave up the ghost in 1975. The final Deep Purple lineup of the '70s featured guitarist Tommy Bolin (who also played wonderfully on Billy Cobham's *Spectrum*) on 1975's *Come Taste the Band.*

Thereafter Paice joined his ex-Purple band mates in Paice, Ashton & Lord, joined Whitesnake for three albums, then turned dirty and lowdown with hard blues guitarist Gary Moore. That gig lasted until 1984, at which time the "classic" Deep Purple returned with *Perfect Strangers* and *The House of Blue Light.* They reprised the effort on 1993's *The Battle Rages On.* And Deep

Purple has just kept on keeping on, practically ever since, hiring guitarist Steve Morse for 1996's *Purpendicular* and '98's *Abandon. Bananas* appeared in 2003.

Throughout his career, Paice has enjoyed copious studio work, including recordings with Velvet Underground, Pete York, Eddie Harris, Elf, Bobby Harrison, Maggie Bell, Kirby, Bernie Marsden, Ken Hensley, Tommy Bolin, Jim Capaldi, Ronnie James Dio, George Harrison, and Paul McCartney.

GEAR & SETUP

Ian Paice's first set was a red glitter $50 Gigster brand kit his dad purchased so his youngster could make club dates with his standards trio. A few months later, with the first proceeds of his endeavors, Paice purchased a professional Premier kit finished in "Aquamarine Pearl." By the time The Beatles struck, Paice invested in a Ludwig Black Oyster Pearl set à la Ringo, complete with Avedis Zildjian cymbals. His affiliation with Ludwig would last until the 1980s, when Pearl became his drum set of choice.

Paice's original Ludwig silver sparkle kit with Deep Purple was a massive affair, including a 6.5×14 snare drum, 14×16 mounted tom, 16×18 and 18×20 floor toms, and a 14×22 bass drum (Buddy Rich on steroids, anyone?). Then as now, these were very unorthodox sizes, but they helped Paice to not only stand out visually but to produce a walloping low-end attack that matched his incredible technical skills. He switched to Ludwig Melodics series drums around the release of *Come Taste the Band*. This set included a massive 26" bass drum, the choice no doubt influenced by John Bonham's titanic *thud*.

Paice's current sticks of choice are Pro-Mark Ian Paice Signatures, and his Paiste cymbal complement includes 15" 2002 Sound Edge hi-hats, 22" 2002 crash, 10" 2002 splash, 22" 2002 Power Ride Custom, 24" 2002 crash, and either a 24" or 22" China Type.

His current Pearl Masters Custom set revolves around his 6.5×14 Ian Paice Signature (brass) Snare Drum, and a big set: 10×10, 10×12, and 11×13 toms, 16×16 and 16×18 floor toms, additional 12×14 and 12×15 toms over his floor toms, and his ever massive 16×26 bass drum (with all Pearl hardware). Some things never change.

Ian's studio kit changes slightly, as do his cymbals. The Pearl maple shell studio kit has a 5×14 free-floating wood snare, 8×10, 10×12, and 11×13 mounted toms, 16×16 and 16×18 floors, and a 16×26 bass drum. His Paiste cymbals are 15" 2002 hi-hats, 22" 2002 ride, 21" and 22" crashes, and 20" or 22" China Type.

Remo Coated Ambassador heads top off all his drums, top and bottom, except the bass drum, which is outfitted with Remo Fibreskin III heads and a Remo Muff'l. There is no damping of snare or toms.

Paice always sat slightly high off the set and tuned his drums to the standard rock tuning of the day. "The only thing I tune high is the snare drum,"

Paice told Drumnet.co.uk. "It has to be clean. You have to find that balance where you've got hit and impact and also the clarity."

Paice also went for a balanced sound with his toms, focusing on "hearing the weight." Given a choice between fast response and a booming sound, Paice went for the bigger sound every time. Paice is renowned for his blisteringly fast rolls, so it is surprising that he still considers sound, not technique, to be his main concern. This came no doubt from his love of big band drummers, who pioneered big-stage volume before the advent of rock amplification.

STYLE & TECHNIQUE

As one who taught himself to play the drums beyond his father's basic double stroke instruction, Paice found novel ways to make the rudiments his own. For instance, he found that by accenting different parts of the individual rudiments he could assert his own personality and develop interesting patterns and rhythms to apply to the set. His double paradiddle execution between the two mounted toms on the track "Chasing Shadows" (1969's *Deep Purple*) is one example of this.

CHECKLIST ✓

❑ Drums
1970s Ludwig silver sparkle kit, 2000s Pearl Masters Custom Extra

❑ Condition
New

❑ Sticks
Pro-Mark Ian Paice Signature

❑ Setup
Sits slightly high, enabling massive power strokes

❑ Effects
Cowbell, timbales

❑ Feel
Extroverted, swinging, dazzling, funky, pushing the beat

❑ Signature traits
Blazing single-stroke rolls, sizzling buzz rolls, agitated cowbell funk, big-band-style tom/snare combinations, full set triplets

❑ Influences
Gene Krupa, Buddy Rich, Ginger Baker, Carmine Appice, Mitch Mitchell, Ringo Starr, Bernard Purdie

❑ Overall approach
Like Buddy Rich playing hard rock, Ian Paice lent an air of extroverted flash and funky bombast to the proto heavy metal of Deep Purple, turning their powerful blues derived primitivism into an overheated drag race of smoke, sparks, and fire

SELECTED DISCOGRAPHY

With Deep Purple:

In Rock
Machine Head
Live in Japan
Who Do We Think We Are
Burn
Stormbringer
Come Taste the Band

With Whitesnake:

Ready an' Willing
Come an' Get It
Saints and Sinners

With Gary Moore:

Corridors of Power
Victims of the Future
Rockin' Every Night
We Want Moore

RECOMMENDED CUTS

"Highway Star" (*Machine Head*)
"Space Truckin'" (*Machine Head*)
"Fireball" (*Fireball*)
"Burn" (*Burn*)
"Speed King" (*In Rock*)
"Lay Down, Stay Down" (*Burn*)
"Sail Away" (*Burn*)
"Might Just Take Your Life" (*Burn*)
"Living Wreck" (*In Rock*)
"You Fool No One" (*Burn*)
"Dealer" (*Come Taste the Band*)

Though he is self-taught, Paice believes everyone can use a teacher. "If you have a teacher in your area, learn the basics and then forget it," he told *Modern Drummer* magazine in 1984. "Learning the basics will save you five or six years of struggling to find them all over again once you think you can play. It's a very destructive thing to think you've been playing five or six years and you can't play. There are things you just don't know how to do, and they're so simple when somebody shows you how to do them."

But he also suggests that young drummers play with records. "Play whatever turns you on when you listen to a record until you know how to do it, or until what you do sounds better than the record. The great thing about teaching yourself is that you learn very quickly what does not work. Listening to records helps you formulate your own style too because you're not listening to one person. You're drawing from three or four, and adding whatever you think is slightly better. That way, you become your own person."

And Paice also offered a couple of tips in that same article. "The simplest one," he recommended, "is being able to perfect the daddy-mommy between the snare drum and the bass drum. If you get the placing of the notes right on two bass drums, it gives your hands time to do independent things and the sound never stops. It's the sort of thing that people need two bass drums to do. You never develop that devastating power that two bass drums can have. You can fool so many people with what you're doing because you have so much speed going. But when you've just got one foot, nobody can see how you can get two or three notes happening by sliding your foot forward on the bass drum pedal."

One instance where Paice opted for double bass over a single bass drum was on 1971's "Fireball." Though the intro originally began with Paice using one bass drum, he really wanted the powerful assault only two bass drums could provide. The Who had been recording the night before in the same studio, and Keith Moon's double bass Premier kit was still set up. So Paice dragged one of Moon's bass drums over and replicated his single bass drum part on two bass drums. As he has often said, he never tried to hide the fact that he used two bass drums on "Fireball" instead of his usual single-bass setup. But even now Paice claims it is relatively easy to imitate the sound of two bass drums. It's all about using the listeners' pre-conceived notions about the bass drum always landing on the downbeat to fool them into hearing something that isn't really there. Instead of starting with the bass drum on the *one*, Paice prescribes, you play the "an" (or second eighth-note) of every beat. With the ensuing music the listener may *think* he hears a second bass drum, until you he actually hears someone play the same track with two bass drums. Sleight of hand equals sleight of foot?

Ian Paice's drumming also contains a certain magical, indefinable quality that is nearly impossible to replicate. His best drumming sounds almost compressed, or supercharged from the inside out, as though each note is fired by some invisible piston. There is tremendous power in his every stroke, giving grooves, fills, and accents a trademark surge of energy that is unlike that of any other drummer from the '70s, Bonham included. But every note is delivered with great ease and sense of flow. Paice knew exactly where to gauge and distribute the intensity of each rhythm and accent for maximum impact. Simply said, his drumming is enough to take your head off.

A prime example of this is "Burn," from the album of the same name. An up-tempo track, it begins with a raunchy Gilmore guitar intro and a cymbal crash from Paice, his pumping hi-hat keeping time in the background. He quickly answers the guitar with pounding eighth-notes played in unison on the toms, before a crunchy single-stroke roll fires from snare to tom into the verse, the organ joining in the fury. The main beat is a simple *two* and *four* smash, with single and double syncopated strikes on the bass drum, but the power and sheer propulsion of Paice's groove sets the song in motion like a pillaging army. It is impossible to imagine anyone else playing this song but Ian Paice. David Coverdale sings, "The sky is red," igniting Paice into a flurry of single-stroke rolls assaulting the toms, snare, and floor tom, and this all in the space of the first 16 bars! Paice continues to flail over the verse with cymbal/bass drum smashes, intense tom and snare singles, and one particularly burning buzz roll that roars through a full bar then smacks hard on the downbeat of *one* to set up the chorus. It's an amazing bit of drum theater, and will exhaust most drummers just trying to figure out what is passing before their eyes. But Paice sounds typically at ease, executing this demanding foray with energy to, well, burn. His manic but controlled energy continues for the rest of the song, the flailing rolls returning at the head of each verse. Paice consistently finds new ways to push the song, bashing the hi-hat through the verses and guitar solo, crashing the cymbal with guitar/organ accents, and pressurizing his buzz roll like an angry weapon throughout.

His drumming is what makes the song work, the intensity level just one step below self-immolation.

Of equal intensity on *Burn* are the irrepressible fire and grandiose fills (check the urgent hi-hat swipes) of "Lay Down, Stay Down," the hard-edged rock-funk of "Sail Away," the funky cowbell mayhem (and quick cymbal clutch) of "You Fool No One," and classic rock strut of "Mistreated."

LESSON

To play like Ian Paice, you need to master the power of a hard-rock pounder and the finesse, technique, and approach of a big-band drummer. Paice set up every figure in the music of Deep Purple as a big-band drummer would, telegraphing section changes with swinging tom fills or single-stroke rolls that struck like heat-seeking missiles. That the self-taught Paice claimed no special technical training is simply a fluke; drummers looking to emulate his combination of speed, power, funk, and full-set skills will need to spend serious hours perfecting all manner of single-stroke and buzz rolls, snare and tom combinations, full-set patterns, and power grooves. Additionally, ear training with the recordings of Ginger Baker (Cream), Mitch Mitchell (Jimi Hendrix Experience), Bernard Purdie (Aretha Franklin), and Buddy Rich (Buddy Rich Big Band) will put the drummer in the correct frame of mind to blow down the walls, Ian Paice style.

Essentials

▶ Rock grooves played with funk pulse
▶ Full-set studies incorporating triplets, flams, and rolls
▶ Complete rudimental snare studies
▶ Studies for speed and dexterity

Example 1

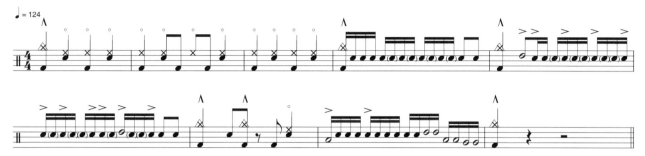

Now all those rudimental studies and metronome workouts pay off. Ian Paice has two of the fastest hands in rock, and this beat will require all the speed and fortitude you can muster. Beyond a blazing press roll into the chorus, the ambitious drummer must be able to execute incredibly fast single-stroke 16th-note rolls and swing triplets. It's Buddy Rich racing for his life, Philly Joe Jones playing the fastest rudiments of his career, and Carl Palmer just holding on for a drink. A basic smash and trash groove is heightened by rolls that in some cases run the entire 16 counts of the bar. Whew!

Example 2

Another hyper, take-no-prisoners beat, delivered in slamming four-to-the-bar fashion. Speedy single-stroke rolls explode like missiles, and big cymbal/ bass drum accents mirror the song's major breaks. Also of note, more 16th-note full-set triplets delivered with startling speed.

Example 3

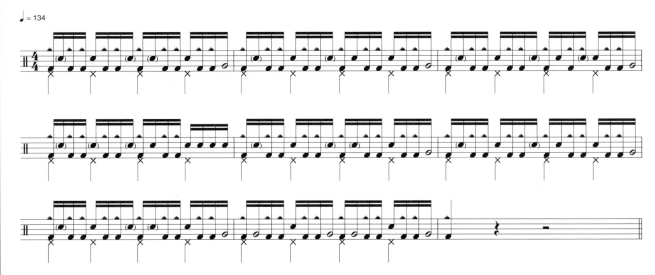

Paice is known for his rock punch, but here he plays it funky with a cowbell/ bass drum rhythm that is the foundation of the song. Paradiddles loosely played with the *R* on the cowbell, in unison with the bass drum and left-hand ghost-notes on the snare, are a good way to master this 16th-note rhythm.

Example 4

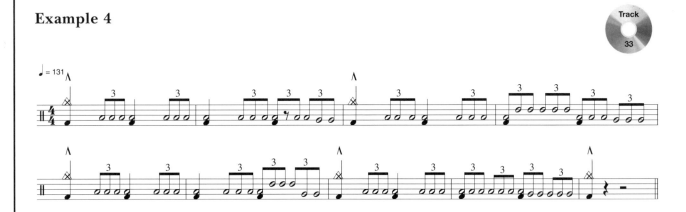

Dropping a tom pop on the "uh" before every other downbeat heightens the level of difficulty—and the fantastic degree of funk.

After Ian Paice's steaming singles and grooves, this double-sticking exercise (modeled on Deep Purple's early hit "Hush") may seem simple, but once you master this slow tempo, ramp it up. It may surprise you.

CHAPTER 9
Jeff Porcaro

When it comes to pure groove, the kind that can float an oil tanker and never leak, the drumming of Jeffrey Thomas Porcaro is unparalleled. He played on thousands of sessions before his tragic death in 1992, and Porcaro's drumming remains the bible every drummer must read, the be-all and end-all of massive groove logic and exemplary feel. And though he constantly berated himself for his self-perceived lack of technique, Porcaro's drumming on records by Steely Dan, Carly Simon, Boz Scaggs, Michael Jackson, Madonna, Jackson Browne, David Gilmour, Mark Knopfler, Donald Fagen, Earth, Wind & Fire, Eric Clapton, Bruce Springsteen, and hundreds of other artists, including his own band, Toto, stands as one of the most individual and inspiring bodies of work found in any style of drumming.

BIOGRAPHY

Born April 1, 1954, in Hartford, Connecticut, to a successful Los Angeles studio percussionist, Joe Porcaro, Jeff was joined by two younger musical siblings, Steve and Mike. All three played drums as children, gathering in the family room to work on their rudiments. An avid drummer by the age of seven, Jeff studied with papa Porcaro as well as LA instructors Bob Zimmitti and Rich Lapore (after the family's move to the West Coast in 1966). Jeff also learned from playing in local bands and with records. After school he would often put on his headphones and play to the incessant soul hit "Boogaloo Down Broadway" by The Fantastic Johnny C. Additionally, Jeff played with Beatles and Jimi Hendrix records, believing that if he perfectly aligned his playing with Ringo Starr and Mitch Mitchell, respectively, he would then understand those same grooves in a live situation. Jeff once spoke of copying Jim Gordon's beat on Steely Dan's "Charlie Freak" for his drumming on Boz Scaggs' "Lido Shuffle." He also claimed to have cloned himself after Jim Keltner during his teenage years between 17 and 18.

While attending Grant High School in Van Nuys, Jeff would cross the street to Valley Junior College to watch their chart-reading big band. Jeff compared chart reading to understanding key words and reading a sentence, though he never claimed to be a great sight reader.

Later, while playing in a local band (Rural Still Life) with keyboardist David Paich and bassist David Hungate (founding members of Toto), Jeff was asked to play at a jazz club on LA's Lankersheim Drive. A contractor from A&M records caught the show and invited Jeff to join a rehearsal big band led by The Carpenters' producer, Jack Daugherty. The band recorded an album on Jeff's first session, playing double drums with his hero Jim Keltner on the 1971 release *Jack Daugherty and the Class of Nineteen Hundred and Seventy One*.

Soon thereafter, Jeff was called to record a free demo at pianist Leon Russell's house in North Hollywood. The session included guitarist Dean Parks and bassist Hungate, who were then in the employ of a famous Hollywood couple. Jeff was asked to join the band, and in May 1972 he left high school for a Las Vegas engagement with California show biz icons Sonny and Cher (pay: $1,500 a week). Jeff would go on to play on their popular TV variety show for two years. Next he hit the road and recorded with Seals and Crofts, and in 1974, as if to signal the diversity that would become his trademark, he landed a coveted spot with the ultimate studio group Steely Dan (after the group's Donald Fagen and Walter Becker caught Jeff live at Dantes in LA). He appeared on Steely Dan's third album, *Pretzel Logic*, and the following releases, *Katy Lied* and *Gaucho*, as well as Fagen's *The Nightfly*. Jeff also double-drummed with original Steely Dan drummer Jim Hodder for a Steely Dan tour in 1974 (the pair would solo on Dan's big hit "Do It Again"). After the stamp of approval given every Steely Dan session player,

Jeff became one of the most in-demand studio drummers in LA, playing with musicians of a thousand different stripes and styles. Jeff's 20-year run of session dates began, and his legend as a drummer with incredible feel and great imagination grew.

After the success of Boz Scaggs' 1978 smash *Silk Degrees*, which featured the songwriting and performing skills of Jeff and his old friends Paich and Hungate, he joined with them to form Toto; the band would soon become a million-selling, Grammy-winning Top-40 act. Toto included other LA session heavyweights in guitarist Steve Lukather, vocalist Bobby Kimball, and Jeff's brother Steve on keyboards. Their 1979 debut single, "Hold The Line," sold millions, followed by a string of AOR (album-oriented rock) hits, including "Africa," "Rosanna," "I Won't Hold You Back," "I'll Be Over You," and "Without Your Love." Toto IV dominated the Grammies in 1982, winning in multiple categories. Toto continued to chart hit singles through the latter '80s, but their albums didn't fare quite as well.

CHECKLIST ✓

❏ Drums
Pearl Masters Series Maple, Paiste cymbals

❏ Condition
New

❏ Sticks
Regal Tip Jeff Porcaro model

❏ Setup
Sits even with snare drum, with drums practically wrapping around him like a European sports car, cymbals set high

❏ Effects
Dynacord electronic drums, occasional hand drums and percussion

❏ Feel
Variable depending on situation, but primarily a deep and powerful pulse

❏ Signature traits
Brilliantly smooth hi-hat work, powerful earth-rocking grooves, giant flam-based tom fills, spidery full-set patterns, ability to fuse with any style

❏ Influences
Jimi Hendrix, Jim Keltner, Jim Gordon, Joe Porcaro

❏ Overall approach
The ultimate studio drummer (a term he hated), Porcaro could adapt to any style and quickly master its complexities and subtleties; he would give his all for any musician, feeling he was a kindred artist at heart

SELECTED DISCOGRAPHY

With Toto:
Toto
Toto IV
Fahrenheit

With Boz Scaggs:
Silk Degrees
Down Two Then Left

With James Newton Howard:
James Newtown Howard and Friends

With Steely Dan:
Katy Lied
Pretzel Logic
Gaucho

With Donald Fagen:
The Nightfly

With Los Lobotomys:
Lobotomys

With Les Dudek:
Say No More

RECOMMENDED CUTS

"FM" (*Gold*)
"Gaucho" (*Gaucho*)
"Your Gold Teeth II" (*Countdown to Ecstasy*)
"Daddy Don't Live in That New York City No More" (*Katy Lied*)
"Doctor Wu" (*Katy Lied*)
"Bad Sneakers" (*Katy Lied*)
"Night by Night" (*Pretzel Logic*)
"Beat It" (*Thriller*)
"Africa" (*Toto IV*)
"99" (*Hydra*)
"Hold the Line" (*Toto IV*)
"Rosanna" (*Toto IV*)
"The Goodbye Look" (*The Nightfly*)
"Love Me Tomorrow" (*Silk Degrees*)
"Harbor Lights" (*Silk Degrees*)
"Gone Buttefishin" (*James Newton Howard and Friends*)
"Slippin' Away" (*James Newton Howard and Friends*)

As Toto's success faltered, Jeff continued to track sessions with an extremely wide array of artists. His session credits on recordings released between 1988 and 1998 include Robben Ford, Michael Feinstein, Randy Newman, Barbra Streisand, Don Henley, Larry Carlton, Madonna, Sergio Mendes, Dire Straits, Manhattan Transfer, Bonnie Raitt, 10CC, Bruce Springsteen, Les Dudek, Gene Clark, and Jeff Berlin.

It all came to end on August 5, 1992, when Jeff died of a heart attack due to an allergic reaction to pesticides while working in the garden of his Sherman Oaks home. Porcaro's funeral service at the Forest Lawn Memorial Park in Hollywood five days later included a loop of four songs: Steely Dan's "Third World Man," "Home At Last," and "Deacon Blues," and Jimi Hendrix's "The Wind Cries Mary." Jeff Porcaro was 38.

GEAR & SETUP

Jeff Porcaro played many, many different drum and cymbal setups during his career, usually using Pearl drums and Paiste cymbals for his later years with Toto. His first set was a Slingerland champagne sparkle four-piece that a friend's father had won in a poker game, which his dad bought for $250. Sizes were a 5×14 snare, 8×12 and 16×16 toms, 22" bass drum and 20" and 18" cymbals. By the late '70s Jeff was using three different Ludwig sets, a Camco set, and two Gretsch sets. Two of the Ludwig kits consisted of 22" bass drums, 9×13, 10×14, 16×16, and 18×18 toms. The third Ludwig set included a 24" bass drum, 8×12 and 9×13 mounted toms, and a 16×18 floor tom. His Gretsch kits were outfitted with 8×12 and 9×13 toms, 16×16 floor toms, and an 18" bass drum, the second set changing slightly: 7×10, 8×12, and 14×14 toms. His Camco (now Drum Workshop) set featured a 24" bass drum, 8×12 and 9×13 toms, 16×16 and 18×18 floor toms. He used the Ludwigs as his all-around set, and the Gretsch for live performances. Ludwig heads were used on his toms and Remo Ambassadors for the snare drum.

Jeff's snare drum tuning for the studio was quite intense. "As far as snare drums go," he told *Modern Drummer* in 1978, "I use a 6.5 Ludwig metal snare with the bottom head pretty tight and the snares going all the way across. I put the top head on and use a splicing block, like those used for splicing tape, or something about that size. I put it together with some foam, and I wrap a piece of leather around and lay it so the foam is resting against the head. A wallet sounds good on top of the snare. The top head is tuned loose to where each lug is about to fall off. Start hitting it with the snares real loose and raise the pitch of the head from that position, tightening the snares slightly. Within about three rotations, you've got yourself a nice sounding snare drum. I keep the top heads loose and the bottom heads tight on my toms to get the pitch to bend a little."

By the '80s and super-arena rock, Porcaro switched to Pearl drums and Paiste cymbals for Toto tours. His 1982 tour kit comprised a 6.5×14 Slingerland Radio King snare, 8×10, 10×12, and 11×13 toms, and a 16×16 floor tom, all Pearl Maple Shells. Cymbals were Paiste 2002 series, 14" hi-hats, (2) 19" and 21" crashes, 22" ride, and 20" China type. By 1987 he had switched to Yamaha and Brady snares and Pearl MLX drums. Both his drums and cymbal complements grew larger to accompany Toto's increasingly broadening sound palette. Jeff also used Dynacord ADD-One electronic drums and Dynacord pads for large gong and timbale sounds.

STYLE & TECHNIQUE

Jeff Porcaro never claimed to have great technique—quite the contrary. He was known to throw his sticks against the wall and leave in disgust if he had trouble with a particular song (he walked out of a Rickie Lee Jones session when she singled him out for undue criticism; he also sent a Linn drum in his place after one producer demanded he play with a canned band loop). But his consummate skill, passion for recording, deep-as-the-ocean groove, and inherent musicality belied his self-effacing attitude. A hundred drummers could probably execute Jeff's trademark patterns in such classic tracks as Toto's "Rosanna," "Lowdown," and "Africa," Steely Dan's "Doctor Wu," and Boz Scaggs' "Love Me Tomorrow" and "Lido Shuffle," but none could infuse them with his sense of grace, his dynamic shading of the pulse, and his massive time feel. Jeff's shuffle beat was beyond compare in such songs as "Lido Shuffle," "Rosanna," and "Black Friday," but he could also play over the bar line (Steely Dan's "Gaucho"), samba (Fagen's "Goodbye Look"), reggae (Toto's "Somewhere Tonight," "Til the End"), neo-jazz (Steely Dan's "Your Gold Teeth II"), power rock (Toto's "Hold the Line"), and delicate ballads (Scaggs' "Harbor Lights"). His versatility and sensitivity in every situation made Jeff a first-call musician for every genre of music.

Much of Jeff's style lay in his diverse approach to every session. He was dedicated to getting the best track possible, no matter the cost. For Steely

Dan's swinging 3/4 jazz waltz (including accents emphasizing 6/4 and 9/4) "Your Gold Teeth II," Jeff listened to Charles Mingus' records, particularly to his drummer, Dannie Richmond. Copying Richmond's angular jazz playing, Jeff captured the feel Fagen was looking for, but not without difficulty. Easily the toughest track on Katy Lied, "Your Gold Teeth II" required many takes on successive nights. By the seventh night the band nailed it.

For Boz Scaggs' million-selling "Lowdown" single, Jeff copied a groove from Earth, Wind & Fire's *I Am*. After laying down a basic eighth-note shuffle beat, Jeff double-tracked 16th hi-hat notes over his own slightly behind-the-beat groove. Jeff's silky hi-hat work was a trademark that continued to expand and evolve. He played beautifully concise reggae for another track on *Silk Degrees*, the laid-back "Love Me Tomorrow." Here, Jeff does what he called a "bad imitation of Bernard Purdie" on King Curtis' "Memphis Soul Stew." More of Jeff's silky hi-hat can be heard on Toto's "Georgy Porgy," where he plays a right-hand-executed 16th-note hi-hat pulse with a gorgeous R&B flow in the style of Earth, Wind & Fire's Maurice and Freddie White and Paul Humphrey.

"Africa" was one of Toto's biggest hits, based around Jeff's primally hypnotic, 16th-note full-kit pattern. This was one of the first instances of a cut-up drum loop that felt great.

"When we were doing 'Africa,'" Porcaro told *Modern Drummer* magazine in 1988, "I set up a bass drum, snare drum and a hi-hat, and percussionist Lenny Castro set up beside me on conga. We started playing the basic groove, bass drum on 1, the 'and' of 2, and 3. The backbeat is on 3, so it's a half-time pattern. We played for five minutes on tape, no click, no nothing. I was singing the bass line so we had a relative tempo. Afterwards, we picked out the best two bars that we thought were grooving, and marked the two bars on tape. And we made another four bars before those two bars. Then with a cowbell and a shaker we played on two new tracks and they gave us a cue when the first mark went by. We began playing so we were locked into the groove and we overdubbed the percussion. We cut the tape and made a one bar loop of all the instruments together. Then David Paich and I played piano and drums, respectively, over the tape. When we got to the fill before the chorus, I started playing the chorus and when the verse or intro came back, I stopped playing. Then I added bongos and big shakers doing quarter notes, stacking two tracks of sleigh bells, two tracks of big jingle sticks, and two tracks of tambourine all to one track. [He also added a 20×20 revolutionary-war-type rope drum on the downbeat.] I was trying to get the sounds I would hear in a *National Geographic* special."

Steely Dan's "Gaucho," from the album of the same name, is a perfect example of Jeff's ability to add a sense of plushness to any groove, even one as enigmatic and time-tumbling as this. Though "Gaucho" is in 4/4 time, its chorus constantly rearranges the time, placing the melody over the bar line and adding unusual accents. The result is perfectly seamless, Jeff's time and consequently the entire track projecting an almost eerily glistening pulse. Steely Dan is renowned for its ability to make studio players sweat, but that only made Jeff work harder. He initially approached the track as a bolero, breaking up the rhythm between the ride cymbal and snare.

"We were recording tracks for Steely Dan's *Gaucho* at A&R," producer Gary Katz told *Drum* magazine. "In those days, we would record tracks forty, fifty, sixty times until Donald [Fagen] felt he had a track that was steady enough. We didn't use click tracks, and the kind of click track that was available, Jeffrey hated."

After Fagen left the studio dissatisfied with the initial takes for the title track, Porcaro and Katz spent the rest of the night (from 11:00 p.m. to 5:00 a.m.) trying to build a rock steady track, literally from the bottom up. The pair recorded almost 70 takes, the engineer and drummer picking out a bar here, a bar there, which they hoped would result in a drum track the demanding Fagen would accept. The following morning, Katz, Porcaro, and fellow engineer Roger Nichols assembled at the studio and edited all the best bits together to create a single track. Later that day Fagen and Becker signed off on "Gaucho," perhaps never knowing the painstaking and sleepless process the song had required.

Ultimately, "Gaucho" required 46 separate tape edits to meet Porcaro and Katz's high standards. Chalk up another brilliant track to that famous Porcaro persistence. (Odd fact: Jeff's favorite track with Steely Dan was not the time-twisting "Gaucho" or even the odd-metered "Your Gold Teeth II," but the simple eighth-note rock gem "FM." Odd fact #2: Jeff played on the first record with electronic drums to become a hit single, Carly Simon's "Nobody Does It Better".)

Another Porcaro trademark is his subtle yet powerful hi-hat work. As already mentioned, he knew how to get the best out of the hats, as in "Lowdown" and the smooth-as-silk flow of "Georgy Porgy," but as his career progressed he developed greater degrees of finesse and creativity. Check Toto's "99," where he changes the pressure on the hi-hat to accompany the song's flowing moods, and the entire session for Boz Scaggs' *Down Two Then Left*, which is some of Jeff's slickest work, bar none. Jeff knew when to use different parts of the stick to change colors on the hats, or simply opened and closed the hat to add texture.

Another trademark was his propulsive full-set patterns, such as on 1985's *James Newton Howard and Friends*, a startling record of free-flowing LA fusion. (Howard's soundtrack to *Glengarry Glen Ross* also finds Jeff swinging like mad.)

LESSON

Regarding session work, Porcaro told *Modern Drummer,* "to be completely aware of the song; try to hear the song as many times as possible and play for the song not for yourself or for whomever else. Show up early, work with the engineer to tune your drums and look at the [music] ahead of time in case it's something that's too hard for you to do so you can woodshed. Be polite… don't do dope…certain drugs affect some people's time or their concentration or their attitude."

Essentials

- ▶ Rudimental studies focusing on single-stroke rolls and flams
- ▶ Playing ahead of, in the middle of, and behind the beat
- ▶ Odd meter studies
- ▶ 4/4 grooves with an emphasis on full-set integration, swing, Latin, and rock styles
- ▶ Flam patterns played as fills on snare and toms
- ▶ Rudimental studies on hi-hat

Example 1

This cut-time beat is very deceptive. Playing the funky rock bass drum pattern against a simple eighth-note triplet hi-hat groove is one thing. But Porcaro streamlined the whole work with sophisticated eighth-note triplets between the hi-hat and snare, giving the beat a shuffling, silken feel that remains one of his crowning achievements. Practice the basic groove and the internal eighth-note triplets (two eighth-note triplets per quarter-note) separately, then combine them—slowly! The results will be worth the sweat.

Example 2

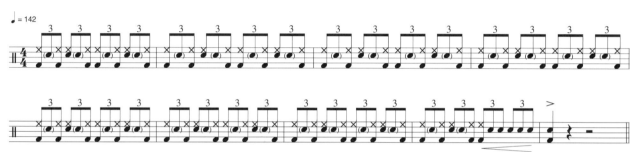

Jeff's other trademark was his fantastic shuffle beat, as heard on "Black Friday," "Lowdown," and here in "Lido Shuffle." Jeff once again mixes in ghost-notes with a shuffling hi-hat/snare pattern, and the bass drum is played very tightly and in near unison.

Example 3

Ah, Jeff could do it all, here playing one of the most beautiful 16th-note hi-hat R&B patterns ever recorded. Instead of playing a static 16th-note hi-hat pulse, play 16ths accenting the eighths, breaking up the pattern with accents as you rock your wrist to maintain the flow (and ease the lactic acid!).

Example 4

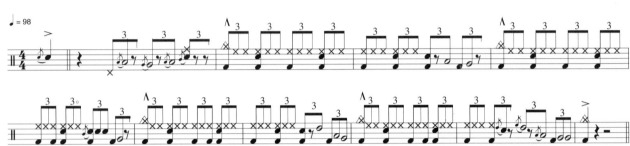

Porcaro played so many great fills: the reggae explosions of "Somewhere Tonight," the slick timbale attacks of "FM" (Steely Dan) and "Love Me Tomorrow" (Boz Scaggs), the nail-biting Latin figures that close "Dr Wu" (Steely Dan). Here is an example of his heavy rock style circa Toto's 1978 debut. Flams, big tom fills, four-to-the-floor grunt.

CHAPTER 10
Ringo Starr

The Beatles' drummer Ringo Starr will forever be remembered for his shaking head of moptop hair and clownish demeanor. But beyond his good-natured appeal, Starr's contribution to the world's most influential rock 'n' roll band was very creative and highly individual, mirroring The Beatles' diverse songs with surprisingly clever and resourceful drumming in a groove that felt as comfortable as an old brown shoe.

BIOGRAPHY

Born Richard Starkey on July 7, 1940, in Liverpool's tough Dingle section, Ritchie, as he was affectionately called, was a sweet but often sick child who was afflicted almost yearly with near fatal illnesses that caused him to lag behind in his schoolwork, causing him to grow increasingly introverted and sensitive. Ritchie's stepfather, Harry Graves, gave him his first set of drums, a cheap kit that was soon replaced by a professional Premier model. With bad grades preventing him from entering a trade school (as was the practice in '50s London), Ritchie gravitated toward the then popular skiffle craze and joined his first band, the Eddie Clayton Skiffle Group.

From 1957 to 1959, Ritchie's reputation as a drummer grew as he played with a variety of bands such as the Darktown Skiffle Group, Al Caldwell's Texans, and the ever popular Rory Storm and the Hurricanes. With his flashy attire, streak of prematurely gray hair, and shiny collection of rings, Richard Starkey became Ringo, photos from the period revealing his quick grin and comic persona in full flower (his solo portion of the Hurricanes' show was billed as "Starr Time"). By 1960, powered by Ringo's steady and swinging beat, Rory Storm and the Hurricanes were Liverpool's top beat group.

The Beatles were another popular Liverpool group whose then drummer, Pete Best, was fired on the verge of their contract-signing with EMI Records. Ringo and Beatles guitarist George Harrison were already close friends from the two bands' joint gigs in Hamburg, Germany, so when Best was ousted, Ringo was the only call for the vacant drum chair. His first gig with The Beatles was a mere 18 days before their EMI recording session.

Practically overnight, The Beatles became England's best-selling group. On the strength of a tremendous run of #1 singles, The Beatles were set to conquer the world. Starr's personable drumming style is evident even on their earliest recordings, *Please Please Me* and *With The Beatles*, displaying Ringo's tasteful use of big-band-style swing triplets, Motown influenced groove patterns, and exhilarating rock 'n' roll feel.

As The Beatles' songwriting matured and expanded, so did Ringo's drumming. He always managed to find the perfect groove, fill, or pattern to every song, setting the mood with unusual cymbal embellishments and tom-tom punctuations or creating beats that became as integral to the songs as the lyrics or guitar parts. A true team player, Ringo never overshadowed the songs but seamlessly integrated his role as both supportive member and rhythmic colorist.

Ringo's drum parts were nearly perfect and typically shrewd. The Beatles' vast influences, which began with British music hall and American R&B then broadened to include avant-garde, Indian, hard rock, jazz, big band, blues, country, and folk, were matched, song for song, by Ringo's chameleon-like performances. Need some shuffle brushwork for Paul McCartney's "When I'm Sixty Four"? No problem. Swaggering heavy metal pummel for John Lennon's

"She's So Heavy" or Paul's "Helter Skelter"? How 'bout western swing for "All My Loving," proto-funk for "Birthday," or Afro-Cuban for "I Feel Fine"? Ringo had all the bases covered. His tom-tom fills are utterly unique—rolling, swinging, slightly behind-the-beat figures heard to perfect effect in "A Day in the Life" and "With a Little Help from My Friends." Couple Ringo's talent for diversity with his ability to navigate John Lennon's odd meter obsessions ("Yer Blues," "All You Need Is Love"), and the case can be made that he was basically a very skilled session drummer in a self-contained band.

Oddly enough, Ringo's contributions still go unrecognized by those who only see worth in flash and fire, but as his landmark drumming in such songs as "Come Together," "Day Tripper," "Rain," "Ticket to Ride," "Tomorrow Never Knows," or his own "It Don't Come Easy" confirms, Ringo Starr is the quiet man with the very large talent.

GEAR & SETUP

Ringo's Ludwig Super Classic Oyster Black Pearl set, with its large *The Beatles* logo on the bass drum head, is one of rock's enduring iconic images. His first few months in the band found him playing a mahogany Premier kit, which

CHECKLIST ✓

❑ **Drums**
Premier 54, Ludwig Super Classic and Hollywood models

❑ **Cymbals**
Paiste, then Zildjian

❑ **Condition**
Broken in, same set for six years

❑ **Sticks**
Regal Tip

❑ **Setup**
Sits high off of set

❑ **Effects**
Maracas, tambourine, congas, bongos, marimba, timpani

❑ **Feel**
Laid back but can become raucous

❑ **Signature traits**
Tumbling tom fills, irregular stickings, broken cymbal patterns, inventive beats

❑ **Influences**
Skiffle, early rock 'n' roll, big band

❑ **Overall approach**
Highly versatile to match style of song

SELECTED DISCOGRAPHY

With The Beatles:

With The Beatles
Please Please Me
Help
Revolver
Sgt. Pepper's Lonely Hearts Club Band
Magical Mystery Tour
Abbey Road

With George Harrison:

All Things Must Pass

With John Lennon:

Plastic Ono Band

Solo album:

A Blast from Your Past

RECOMMENDED CUTS

"With a Little Help from My Friends" (*Sgt. Pepper's Lonely Hearts Club Band*)
"Rain" (*The Beatles: Past Masters Volume Two*)
"A Day in the Life" (*Sgt. Pepper's Lonely Hearts Club Band*)
"And I Love Her" (*A Hard Day's Night*)
"Tomorrow Never Knows" (*Revolver*)
"All You Need Is Love" (*Magical Mystery Tour*)
"It Don't Come Easy" (*Blast from Your Past*)
"She Loves You" (*The Beatles: Past Masters Volume One*)
"The End" (*Abbey Road*)
"Come Together" (*Abbey Road*)
"Here, There and Everywhere" (*Revolver*)
"Everybody's Got Something to Hide Except Me and My Monkey" (*The White Album*)
"Long, Long, Long" (*The White Album*)

also made brief appearances on The Beatles' first two albums. The Premier kit consisted of a 4×14 snare drum, 8×12 tom, 20×16 floor tom, and 17×20 bass drum, and Premier Super Zyn cymbals. But from '64 to 1968 the Ludwig Super Classic set, with its four-ply maple and American veneer shells, was a staple of all Beatles recordings. Ringo's first Ludwig kit was smaller than standard for the period simply so the short-ish Ringo could be seen. The set included a 5.5×14 Jazz Festival snare drum, 8×12 mounted tom, 14×14 floor tom, and a 14×20 bass drum (with foldout bass drum spurs). Later he would upgrade to larger, more standard sizes (9×13, 16×16, 14×22).

Drum heads were usually Remo medium-coated white batter Ambassadors, though Ringo used various-weight bass drum heads, including Ludwig Weather Master and Remo Weather King models. The focus on Weather reflects an earlier generation of calfskin heads that were always at the mercy of temperature conditions.

Ringo's Ludwig hardware included a Speed King No. 201 bass drum pedal and a Speed King hi-hat stand, Flat Base Cymbal Stand No.1400, Rogers Swiv-O-Matic drum-mount system (many drummers, including Ginger Baker, used Rogers hardware with their Ludwig drums, believing the jazz-oriented brand to be stronger), Ludwig Tom Tom Floor Stand No.1345-1 (used in later years), and a Porto-Seat No.1025 drum throne. Ringo used various percussion instruments with The Beatles, including maracas, tambourine, marimba, timpani, conga, and bongos.

Early on Ringo played Paiste cymbals, but after The Beatles' first U.S. tour he switched to Zildjian. Ringo's cymbal dimensions remained constant throughout The Beatles' recordings: 14" or 13" hi-hats, 16" or 18" crashes, and an 18" or 20" ride.

For the 1969 sessions, *Let It Be* and *Abbey Road*, Ringo finally replaced the Oyster Pearl Super Classics with Ludwig's Hollywood Series set with Maple Cortex finish and a chrome Supra-Phonic 400 snare drum (which Ringo preferred not to use). Dimensions remained the same with the addition of an 8×12 rack tom. As can be seen in *Let It Be*, Ringo often covered his heads with towels or pillowcases to muffle the ring and give his sound a deeper tone.

STYLE & TECHNIQUE

Before you can understand Ringo's technique you must consider his *sound*. While most rock 'n' roll and pop drum sounds in the early '60s were still influenced by big band, surf, and jazz, Ringo's sound, typical at first, soon became deeper and more expressive, following The Beatles' lead. Ringo's drums were tuned lower, the toms and snare sometimes covered in a towel for a deader, less ringing sound. Ringo's fat tom sounds and delicate cymbal work were imitated by thousands of drummers. Part of Ringo's sound came from his excellent use of dynamics. He never pounded or overpowered the drums but always played with a complementary volume level (learn and listen!). Ringo (along with Ginger Baker) also popularized the match grip, in contrast to the traditional grip favored by the ruling jazz drummers of the day. And while his level of technical proficiency was not masterful (though he had very quick hands), his ideas and musicality most certainly were.

Early Beatles recordings show Ringo playing fairly conventional beats influenced by R&B and Broadway show tunes, but he was a very versatile musician, having been required to play all manner of rhythms for dances and shows at England's Butlin's Holiday Camp, a forerunner of Disney World. Swing, bossa nova, Latin, rock 'n' roll, waltzes, even twist grooves, were all given life by Ringo's naturally propulsive and big-hearted feel. In The Beatles' *Ed Sullivan* performances, Ringo's mammoth beat and natural sense of flow are what give the band its spark. His musicality was his main resource, turning what could have been stumbling fills and plodding grooves into drumming templates still used by everyone from Jim Keltner to Dave Grohl.

Ringo's loping time feel was the heart of The Beatles' sound, though his literal meter could change drastically within a song to suit the mood of the music. The bridge to "I Want to Hold Your Hand," for instance, is slower than the verse/chorus. The same holds true for "Michelle," "The Night Before," and others. That kind of ebb and flow is now obtained with computer programs, but Ringo did it as naturally as the rain. Ringo's steady pulse enabled The Beatles to splice together various session takes into one song even when odd meters were present, as on "Yer Blues" or the manic cross-rhythms of "Everybody's Got Something to Hide Except for Me and My Monkey." The Beatles often recorded dozens of versions of one song, but Ringo's groove and tempo remained constant. This constancy allowed Paul McCartney to stray from simple timekeeping into his revolutionary bass melodies.

Odd meters were present throughout The Beatles' music, from their early fondness for 6/8 and 3/4, to later successful experiments with 7/4 in

"All You Need Is Love," to the mind-blowing sequence of repeating 11/8, 4/4, and 7/8 passages in "Here Comes the Sun." How Ringo mastered these in an era when even most jazz was in 4/4 is a tribute to his talent. He never sounds less than totally relaxed, which is true of all his drumming.

Ringo's trademarks include the bizarre but effective ride cymbal patterns in "Hey Jude" and "I Am the Walrus," the swing tom triplets of "Tell Me Why," which are heard to greater suspense in "A Day in the Life" and "With a Little Help from My Friends," and the overwhelming drum creations of "Come Together," which fuses a 16th-note hi-hat flourish with a spooky round-the-kit drum roll, and "Ticket to Ride," where rich tom sounds and staggered accents provide one of the most arresting and memorable drum tracks in rock. Ringo's ultimate Beatles performance is "Rain," where his eclectic use of across-the-bar-line tom rolls finds expression against backwards vocal loops and phasey, washed out cymbal production.

LESSON

To play like Ringo you must be relaxed. You must also be fluent in full-set swing triplets (for tom rolls), and in styles including swing and jazz, bossa nova, rumba, hard rock, and funk. You must be ready to spin on a dime whether you are asked to play odd meters or percussion and occasionally piano. The nature of Ringo's talent and contributions are hard to measure, but there are clues and a structure to adhere to. I propose lessons based around the following five themes:

Essentials

▶   Tom rolls based on swing triplets
▶   Cymbal patterns (some irregular) based on Afro-Cuban and swing
▶   Odd meters played with a rock pulse
▶   Swing, shuffle, twist, and 3/4 waltz patterns
▶   Rhythmic groups that begin after the downbeat

Example 1

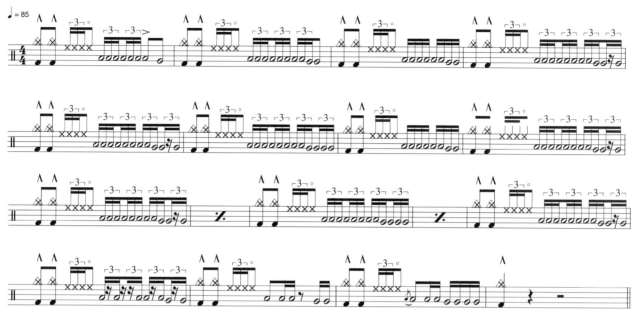

Perhaps Ringo's most creatively daring and technically brilliant groove creation; here he plays rolling quarter-note accents with the bass guitar, then 16th-notes on the hi-hat, slowly opening them as he ends the figure, leading into more 16ths on the toms, creating a descending melodic line that gives the already eerie song an unmistakably downward spiral.

Example 2

Track 39

Ringo's classic tom fills have as their genesis the awesome tom declarations of LA's Hal Blaine, though The Beatles sticks man probably never had him in mind. As always, Ringo came up with the perfect part, perfectly executed. Slightly behind the beat, and played on toms that resonate like mad, these big fills provide a ton of space in the song, adding drama and tension as the song climaxes.

Example 3

More booming swing triplets between snare and toms, with the flow aided by moving the right hand from the hi-hat to the ride cymbal.

Example 4

Who else could have dreamed up the hide-and-seek nature of this quirky beat? Beginning on the bass drum and toms, the focus switches to the cymbal bell, then into the simple groove, and another herky-jerky backwards-moving tom fill. It could only be Ringo.

Example 5

Geoff Emerick's excellent book, *My Life Recording the Beatles*, states that the beat to "Rain" was recorded in half-time, then sped up to the beat we now hear. Hard to believe, as videos of the band show Ringo playing every mad fill and backwards beat with ease, but there you have it. This is Ringo at his most complex, playing jabbing groups of tom fills in unusual phrasings.

Example 6

Variation #1 on above, with looser hi-hat.

Example 7

Variation #2: snare/tom fills that reverse in order (tom/snare) after the first
go-round, with added floor tom and grace notes increasing the flow.

CHAPTER 11
Charlie Watts

If ever simplicity translated into a style, Charlie Watts is a true keeper of the flame. Though Watts' drumming is, on its surface, barely noticeable within the songs of The Rolling Stones, none other than Keith Richards has said that "The World's Greatest Rock and Roll Band" could not survive without Watts' consistently deadpan beat. Like Ringo Starr, who matched ingenious creativity and swinging timekeeping to The Beatles' ever evolving and flowering music, Watts similarly grew as well, his drumming growing in wit and sharpness while The Stones' music never veered from its R&B- and blues-based roots. And though Watts names jazz drummers like Dave Tough and Phil Seaman as his ultimate influences (honestly, his own jazz drumming leaves something to be desired), his unvarying yet unpredictable beat is the stuff of pure rock 'n' roll.

BIOGRAPHY

Born on June 2, 1941, to Charles Richard and Lillian Charlotte Watts in London, Charles Robert Watts trained as a commercial artist and only gave up his day gig when The Rolling Stones secured an eight-month residency at the Crawdaddy Club. Watts' original inspiration to play the drums came when he heard Chico Hamilton playing brushes on "Walking Shoes" with the Gerry Mulligan quartet. Watts practiced rudiments, but never took lessons. He devoured the drumming of Art Blakey, Tony Williams, Dave Tough, Sid Catlett, Buddy Rich, and Danny Richmond. He initially pursued his love for jazz playing in London's East End pubs, and he traveled to Denmark for a few gigs; he even played briefly with Dudley Moore's jazz trio. But soon the R&B and skiffle craze caught his ear, and he landed a gig with Blues by Five, which led to his joining Alexis Korner's band, Blues Incorporated. Korner soon enlisted Mick Jagger, Brian Jones, and Keith Richards, who performed on an infrequent basis with the band. Watts left Korner to work at an advertising agency and was recruited in 1962 to join the then forming Rolling Stones. With the help of manager Andrew Loog Oldham, the Rolling Stones signed to Decca Records, and in June of 1963 released their first single, a cover of Chuck Berry's "Come On." Later that year they hit the charts again with The Beatles' "I Wanna Be Your Man," followed in 1964 by their first successful U.S. single (another cover), Buddy Holly's "Not Fade Away." Billed as the band that wanted to spend the night with you while The Beatles were content to simply hold your hand, The Rolling Stones presented rock 'n' roll's first bad-boy public image, some critics even referring to them as the "Rolling Uglies." Soon the band would have a string of Top Ten U.S. hits and become the biggest challenge to The Beatles' supremacy. "Tell Me (You're Coming Back)," "Time Is on My Side," and "The Last Time" were all smash singles, leading to the Stones' signature song, "(I Can't Get No) Satisfaction," in the summer of 1965. The Stones' blues roots shone through in practically every song, as did their primitive, unadorned rhythms.

Watts' drumming during this early period was largely ordinary, and unrecognizable from that of a thousand beat groups dominating the charts in the early to mid '60s. He played nothing on the level of, say, Ringo's thunderous opening tom-tom shot in The Beatles' "She Loves You" or the magic groove of the Motown drummers. But between 1968 and 1970, Charlie Watts grew into the master stylist we know today.

Between the breakthrough *Beggars Banquet* album and 1969's *Let It Bleed*, the Stones released the massive hit single "Honky Tonk Woman," which marked Charlie Watts' arrival as a drummer who could create signature drum licks that were as important to the band's songs as Keith Richards' ripping guitar or Jagger's yowling vocals. The cowbell-tom introduction to "Honky Tonk Women" is one of the most renowned fills in all of rock 'n' roll, its subtle Latin inflection coupled to a collapsing tom fill that formed the perfect setup to the woozy beat and growling guitar that followed. Watts drives the tune like a long-haul driver putting pedal to metal. On *Let It Bleed*, he came up with another booming opening drum riff in "Monkey Man," then created a virtual drum lexicon of signature beats and fills in the loping tom-snare combinations of "You Can't Always Get What You Want." *Sticky Fingers* (1971) offered further evidence of Watts' growing mastery in "Brown Sugar" and "Bitch," which he drove with a grittily manic intensity. *Exile on Main Street* followed in '72 with another Top Ten single, "Tumbling Dice," which again relied on Watts' flowing fills and chugging beat.

The Stones continued to tour and release hit singles ("Miss You," "It's Only Rock and Roll," "Angie," "When the Whip Comes Down") throughout the '70s and to a lesser degree in the '80s, by which time Watts' heroin addiction became full-blown and took its toll. The band faltered, as did Watts' creativity. The Stones have continued to make music, but the vagaries of time can't be denied.

As The Stones have grown into a geriatric touring act, Charlie Watts has turned his extracurricular attentions to the jazz of his childhood. In 1978 his old band mate and pianist Ian Stewart called upon him to play drums in Rocket 88, a boogie-woogie jazz band that released an album in 1981. Columbia released Watts' *Live at Fulham Hall* in 1986, the album featuring a mammoth big band playing a book of swing-era hits. Watts recorded his quintet covering Charlie Parker tunes for 1991's *From One Charlie* and followed it with *Tribute to Charlie Parker with Strings* later that same year. He continued with a couple of ballad-heavy albums before branching out with fellow drummer Jim Keltner for 2000's *Charlie Watts/Jim Keltner Project*. A full-on tribute album, where each track is named after one of Watts' heroes, from "Art Blakey" to "Tony Williams" to "Billy Higgins," the music is an unusual combination of Watts' sturdy beats and Keltner's oddball percussion, sampling, and sound effects. The album won the pair critical acclaim, though it mostly served to garner more attention for Watts as a solo artist, while giving Keltner a chance to record his large trick bag of toys and effects. In 2004, Watts and his big band recorded *Watts at Scott's*, a live gig at Ronnie Scott's jazz club in London, performing the usual standards repertoire.

In June of 2004 Watts was diagnosed with throat cancer. He underwent radiation therapy and has since recovered and continues his recording and touring role with The Rolling Stones.

GEAR & SETUP

Charlie Watts' first set of Ludwig drums were given to him as a Christmas present when he was 14. But he has stubbornly played the same dimensions and setup of Gretsch drums for more than the 40 years since. His cymbal allegiance has changed from Zildjian to Paiste to Ufip, but the same combination of Gretsch 8×12 tom, 16×16 floor tom (occasionally using an additional

14×14 floor tom), 14×22 bass drum, and 6.5×14 Ludwig Supraphonic snare drum has remained constant. As of the mid '90s, he used a Ludwig Speed King bass drum pedal and a Rogers hi-hat pedal. His cymbals consist of 14" Zildjian hi-hats, an 18" Ufip Chinese cymbal, an 18" Zildjian crash, and 18" flat ride. Brands and dimensions of cymbals have changed through the years only slightly, Watts once saying regarding his basic setup that if it "was good enough for Fred Astaire's drummer it's good enough for me."

Watts never tunes his drums (into the early '00s he still had a Remo Black Dot head on his bass drum), and he hates to overdub in the studio. Everything else is left to the engineer. He uses Vic Firth Charlie Watts Signature Sticks, and no doubt the Vic Firth Jazz Brush.

STYLE & TECHNIQUE

Charlie sits a little high off the kit and ramrod straight. One of the oddest things about Watts' approach is his inability (or predilection not) to play the snare drum and hi-hat in unison when playing the basic eighth-note rock beat. Watts always plays with an awkward, arms-in-choppy-motion style, and he looks strange when playing a beat, lifting his right hand high and away from the hi-hat as he strikes two and four on the snare with his left hand (always

CHECKLIST ✓

❑ **Drums**
Gretsch

❑ **Condition**
Old

❑ **Sticks**
Vic Firth Charlie Watts Signature

❑ **Setup**
Sits high off the set

❑ **Effects**
Cowbell

❑ **Feel**
Pulsing, loose, behind the beat, alternately stomping and stormy

❑ **Signature traits**
Cracking snare drum, booming tom fills, off-kilter hi-hat lead, big-band-influenced funk

❑ **Influences**
Chico Hamilton, Art Blakey, Max Roach, Sid Catlett, Buddy Rich, Phil Seaman

❑ **Overall approach**
A drummer by default, a jazz musician playing rock 'n' roll with an innate understanding of the beauty in simplicity

SELECTED DISCOGRAPHY

With The Rolling Stones:

Sticky Fingers
Exile on Main Street
Steel Wheels
Beggars Banquet
Emotional Rescue
Some Girls

With Jim Keltner:

Charlie Watts/Jim Keltner Project

Solo albums:

Live at Fulham Town Hall
Watts at Scott's

RECOMMENDED CUTS

"Honky Tonk Women" (*Through the Past, Darkly—Big Hits, Vol. 2*)
"Bitch" (*Sticky Fingers*)
"You Can't Always Get What You Want" (*Let It Bleed*)
"Tumbling Dice" (*Exile on Main Street*)
"Loving Cup" (*Exile on Main Street*)

using traditional grip). His grooves are solid, but his technique looks anything but.

There are no great technical secrets or inside tips on the Watts style. At times, he sounds as if he can barely reach the tom and cleanly execute a fill. The magic in Watts' playing is his no nonsense approach. He is very candid about his lack of technique, but the man understands music, and what works. His pulse is the laid-back locomotive backbone of The Stones, his crochety feel and slack strokes recalling great blues drummers like Sam Lay, Willie Smith, and Francis Lay, and Watts knows how to make the music breathe. A thousand drummers try to play like Charlie Watts, usually meaning that they slow their pace, crack their snare drum harder, and generally adopt a sparse approach. But the paradox lies in Watts' ability to drive a band—hard. His simple boom-bap pulse in "Brown Sugar" is perfectly matched to Keith Richards' ragged guitar, the pair working off each other with kinetic intent, heard to great effect in the driving boogie-woogie punch of "Bitch," where Watts doubles Richards' one-two verse accent. Similarly, when Charlie smacks a tumbling three-four eighth-note tom accent in "Let it Bleed," it sounds like the studio walls are ready to crash and burn. Good examples of Watts' intensely popping backbeat are found in "Gimme Shelter," "Rip This Joint," "Jumpin' Jack Flash," and "Sympathy for the Devil." And his greatest fills come alive in "You Can't Always Get What You Want," giant swing triplets slapping the rhythm like a hailstorm, and "Tumbling Dice," a perfect example of Watts creating exquisite, slipping, sliding drum breaks while barely hanging on to the groove. He seems to miss rim shots, his timing is a little off, and he glances cymbals like a blind man, but the performance perfectly matches the song.

LESSON

Playing like Charlie Watts is, as with Keith Moon, perhaps more a state of mind than a state of sticks, but a healthy immersion in the blues of Howlin' Wolf, Muddy Waters, and Junior Wells would be an excellent introduction to the style. Serious rudimental studies are not especially needed, but a strong pulse, ability to swing around the toms, and perfected rim shots are a must. Watts plays the occasional roll, but no more technique than needed to play a slight buzz roll is required.

Essentials

▶ Ruffs, drags, and five-stroke rolls
▶ Rim shots
▶ Swing, shuffle, and eighth-note rock patterns

Example 1

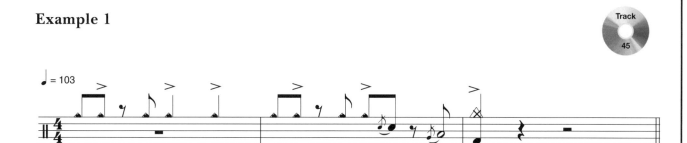

Charlie Watts' classic cowbell intro: a little Latin, a lotta luck, and a massively stumbling tom fill into the groove. The shaky fill that launched a million-selling hit single…

Example 2

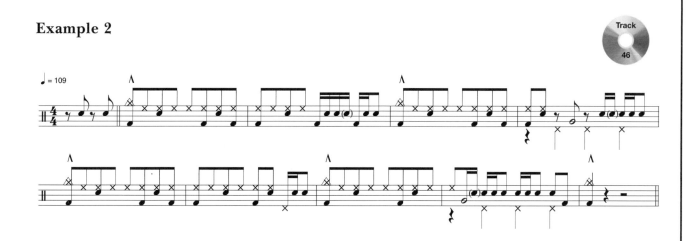

Watts at his most funky and authoritative, dropping eighth-note tom fills before the downbeat and getting all funky to match the looming prowl of Keith Richards' guitar. A tight snap on the snare drum and an equally tight stick on the hi-hat makes this beat work. (Think Al Jackson.)

Example 3

Track 47

Charlie always fancied himself a big-band drummer, and here he comes through, swinging the triplets on the toms like his hero Davey Tough. Drums tuned to ring, low and long, help fill out the note, and a funky, hi-hat-slapping backbeat make the whole thing move like a wild horse. Watts' finest fills ever.

Example 4

Track 48

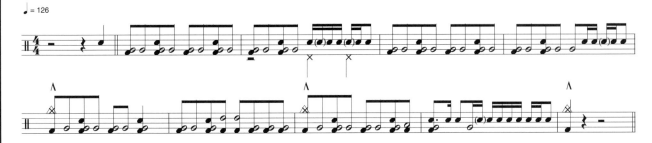

Another big floor-tom-pounding groove, meant to shake up the room and burn down the house. Simplicity is key, with the goal to send the groove popping dead center—not ahead or behind the beat—but right between the eyes.

ACKNOWLEDGMENTS

Ken Micallef thanks Jon and Patti McAuliffe, Sharon Batteau and Andrew Warren, Scott Gloede, Isabel and Ron Spagnardi, and the staff and writers of Modern Drummer magazine: Bill Miller, Adam Budofsky, Rick Van Horn, Robyn Flans, T. Bruce Wittet, Gary Heman, Robin Tolleson, and Scott K. Fish, Joe Castanela, Frank Katz, Zach Danziger, Drummerworld.com, KeithMoon.co.uk, Drumnet.co.uk, Chris Dougherty of Downbeat magazine, Greg Rule of Drum magazine, Povlab.org/Jeff.Porcaro, LedZeppelin.com, Graeme Pattingale, Chris Welch, Chip Stern, Ginger-Baker.com, LevonHelm.com, Backbeat Books, twtd.bluemountains.net.au, Pearldrum.com, Toto99.com, thewho.net/whotabs…moondrums.htm, and especially, Leacy.

Donnie Marshall would like to thank his first drum teacher, the late John Willhelm, for keeping him playing, Frank Jernigan, Jim Brock, Rick Dior, Jim Lackey, Wade Starnes, Sound Source Studios, Bill Hanna, Brian Sullivan, Larry Sharpe, Toni Wicker, Ken Micallef, all his MO $ buddies, all of his students who teach him something new every day, all the musicians that continually inspire him, and especially Kim Carper Marshall for motivation and loving support.

ABOUT THE AUTHORS

Frank Katz

As a drummer for hire during the 1980s and early '90s, **Ken Micallef** toured the East Coast playing pop, jazz, and everything else in between. Micallef attended New York's Drummer's Collective for two years in the '90s before finding a specialist niche as a music journalist. He has written for *Rolling Stone*, *Spin*, and *Billboard*, and is a regular contributor to *Modern Drummer*, *Downbeat*, *Remix*, *Bass Guitar*, 6moons.com, and the Boston *Phoenix*. Ken lives in Manhattan's Greenwich Village, where the sounds on the street can't match the mighty music erupting from his stereo. He currently writes the Yahoo! Music blog Better Living Through MP3 and is also working on his second book, *Jim Gordon: Layla and Other Session Songs.*

Kim Carper Marshall

Donnie Marshall began his career as a professional musician 28 years ago when faced with the decision to either continue his education at Berklee College of Music or stay in his hometown of Charlotte, North Carolina, to perform with and learn from the local greats. He chose the latter, quickly rising through the ranks to become one of the Southeast's most sought-after freelance drummers. Marshall's ability to master all styles of music was borne from more than 10 years of studio work with Sound Choice, the world's largest manufacturer of karaoke CDs and DVDs. Marshall's versatility and professionalism have earned him session and live work with such artists as Aretha Franklin, Ray Charles, Bonnie Bramlett, Ronnie Laws, Gladys Knight, Arthur Smith, The Platters, The Drifters, and many others. Marshall currently maintains a busy schedule of nationwide and local performances and session work, as well as a teaching schedule that includes more than 40 students. He is also the musical director for the NASCAR commentary show Track Side on the Speed Channel.

ON THE CD

Track 1: Ginger Baker Ex. 1

Track 2: Ginger Baker Ex. 2

Track 3: Ginger Baker Ex. 3

Track 4: Ginger Baker Ex. 4

Track 5: John Bonham Ex. 1

Track 6: John Bonham Ex. 2

Track 7: John Bonham Ex. 3

Track 8: John Bonham Ex. 4

Track 9: John Bonham Ex. 5

Track 10: Stewart Copeland Ex. 1

Track 11: Stewart Copeland Ex. 2

Track 12: Stewart Copeland Ex. 3

Track 13: Stewart Copeland Ex. 4

Track 14: Richie Hayward Ex. 1

Track 15: Richie Hayward Ex. 2

Track 16: Richie Hayward Ex. 3

Track 17: Richie Hayward Ex. 4

Track 18: Levon Helm Ex. 1

Track 19: Levon Helm Ex. 2

Track 20: Levon Helm Ex. 3

Track 21: Levon Helm Ex. 4

Track 22: Mitch Mitchell Ex. 1

Track 23: Mitch Mitchell Ex. 2

Track 24: Mitch Mitchell Ex. 3

Track 25: Mitch Mitchell Ex. 4

Track 26: Keith Moon Ex. 1

Track 27: Keith Moon Ex. 2

Track 28: Keith Moon Ex. 3

Track 29: Keith Moon Ex. 4

Track 30: Ian Paice Ex. 1

Track 31: Ian Paice Ex. 2

Track 32: Ian Paice Ex. 3

Track 33: Ian Paice Ex. 4

Track 34: Jeff Porcaro Ex. 1

Track 35: Jeff Porcaro Ex. 2

Track 36: Jeff Porcaro Ex. 3

Track 37: Jeff Porcaro Ex. 4

Track 38: Ringo Starr Ex. 1

Track 39: Ringo Starr Ex. 2

Track 40: Ringo Starr Ex. 3

Track 41: Ringo Starr Ex. 4

Track 42: Ringo Starr Ex. 5

Track 43: Ringo Starr Ex. 6

Track 44: Ringo Starr Ex. 7

Track 45: Charlie Watts Ex. 1

Track 46: Charlie Watts Ex. 2

Track 47: Charlie Watts Ex. 3

Track 48: Charlie Watts Ex. 4

All tracks performed by Donnie Marshall and recorded at Sound Choice Studios, Charlotte, NC.